TROY AIKMAN

★

STEVE YOUNG

TROY
AIKMAN

★

STEVE
YOUNG

RICHARD J. BRENNER

EAST END PUBLISHING, LTD.
SYOSSET, NY

To Jason with love and thanks. And to Halle with love. And with thanks and affection, too, for Janet Speakman, who is always there for me.

And to all the girls and boys in the world, may you always play in happiness.

TROY AIKMAN *STEVE YOUNG

First Printing / July 1994

The cover photo was taken by Robert Tringalli Jr. and supplied by SPORTSCHROME EAST/WEST

Cover design by Steve Bell

Copyright ©1994 by Richard J. Brenner/East End Publishing, Ltd.

Library Systems and Services
Cataloging in Publication Data

Brenner, Richard J., 1941-
    Troy Aikman * Steve Young / Richard J. Brenner.
    p.   cm.
    ISBN 0-943403-26-X

    1. Aikman, Troy, 1966- 2. Young, Steve, 1961-
3. Quarterback (Football)--Biography. I. Title.
GV939.A5B74 1994 796.332'092--dc20

Provided in cooperation with Unique Books, Inc.

This book is published by East End Publishing, Ltd.,
54 Alexander Dr., Syosset, NY 11791

Mr. Brenner is also available to speak to student groups. For details contact East End Publishing, Ltd., 54 Alexander Drive, Syosset, NY 11791, (516) 364-9723.

Contents

TROY AIKMAN

1

Getting Started

Troy Aikman, who was born November 11, 1966, spent the first twelve years of his life in Southern California, first in the city of West Covina and then in the suburb of Cerritos, which isn't much more than a long pass away from Disney Land. Troy, the third child and the first boy born to Charlyn and Kenneth Aikman, liked living in Cerritos, and he loved playing ball. When he lived in Cerritos, Troy concentrated on baseball and basketball; and even back then he was obviously a natural athlete. "Everything I did with sports while I was growing up came easily to me," said Troy.

When Troy was 12, the family moved to a farm near Henryetta, Oklahoma, a small rural community of about 6,000 people. At first, Troy was real unhappy about living in the place he now thinks of as home. "We were eight miles outside of town, on a dirt road. We had suddenly become country folk. It was a big adjustment, a whole different life. But after about four months, I really grew to like it. I came to appreciate that simple lifestyle a lot more, and it felt like I'd lived there all my life."

Given the relative isolation of the ranch and Troy's natural shyness, it took him a little while to make friends in Henryetta. But once school started, Troy's athletic ability and low-keyed personality turned him into the most popular teenager in town. Troy was such a good basketball player that he was able to average more than 20 points per game in his three seasons as a starter for Henryetta High School while leading the Fighting Hens to a District Basketball Championship. "He was real easy to coach," recalled basketball coach Danny Spurlock about the player who was called "Iceman" because of how calm and cool he stayed, even when the games were tight and tense.

And while Troy was a way above average hoopster, he was a true superstar on a baseball diamond. He was such a heavy-hitting shortstop that the people in Henryetta still talk about one massive home run that he hammered so far that it flew over the left field fence and crashed off the wall of a Walmart store almost 400 feet from home plate. But it was Troy's 92 MPH fastball that brought big league scouts to Henryetta and prompted the New York Mets to offer him a $90,000 contract after his senior season with the Fighting Hens. "I really believe I would have played major league baseball if I would have remained in California," said Troy. "But when I moved to Oklahoma, football was bigger there, so my interests started changing."

It would have been unusual for a boy with Troy's athletic abilities not to turn to football once he moved to Oklahoma, where football is *the* sport. But Troy also received a push toward the gridiron from his dad almost as soon as the Aikmans had touched down in Henryetta. "When we moved to Oklahoma I wasn't intending to play football. I was going to play baseball and basketball. But the night they were signing up for eighth-grade football, my dad pulled up and yelled, 'Are you going to play football?' Even though he had never said anything, I knew how much it meant to him. He's a country boy and he likes the toughness of football. So knowing that, I went down there and started playing eighth-grade football."

Troy has always had a lot of respect and admiration for his hard-working father, a man who has earned a living with a blowtorch and a shovel, welding together the pipes that carry gas and water throughout the southwestern United States, from Oklahoma to California. It was from his dad that Troy learned the value of hard work, self-dependence and an inner toughness that sometimes passed the border of good sense. "Once he came home with his finger wrapped in a bandage and wouldn't let anybody look at it," recalled Troy. "Later, we went walking around the farm, working cows, something like that, and I accidentally bumped into his finger. The guy just about fell to his knees in pain.

"I knew this wasn't like him; when he undid the bandage, I discovered that he had chopped off the top part of his finger the day before on the job. It wasn't pretty. The bone was sticking out the end. I rushed him to the emergency room, and the doctor told him he couldn't work for a month and was just about to lose his finger. But my father just asked for an injection and was back at work the next day."

2

Mr. Everything

Although Troy was a year-round athlete, that didn't excuse him from doing regular chores on the farm, or working to earn a few dollars. Troy, in fact, got a firsthand taste of a welder's life as a 13-year-old when his father came home one night and announced that he had arranged for Troy to do some work during the summer. But first, Troy had to meet the man who ran the company and show that he could safely handle a blowtorch. Troy was nervous and uncertain. "I've never welded," he told his dad. "I don't know what to do."

Troy's dad, though, showed him how to wield the tool, and reassured him that he'd do just fine if he put his mind to the task. "My father was always very firm in making me pay attention to what I was taught and not to forget it," said Troy, who passed the test and earned the job.

Troy also spent four years as a part-time worker at the Western Auto store in Henryetta, and like everyone else in town, Jim Lipe, the store's owner, has nothing but nice things to say about him.

"About the only negative thing about Troy was in the selling part of the business. He was a little bit on the shy side in high school, so he wasn't the greatest salesman in the world. But in all the other stuff — the tire changing, mechanical work and stocking the shelves — he would do anything. He was eager to learn; he'd listen and he'd follow instructions."

Troy took that same attitude out to the football field, where there was never any question about his innate talent or his desire to develop it. "When Troy was in the eighth grade, he could stand flat-footed and throw a football 65 yards," recalls John Walker, a former teammate of Troy's and the current coach of the Henryetta High School Football team. "But as talented as he was, you'll never find anybody who worked harder than Troy."

Ish Kaniatobe, an assistant coach who worked with the quarterbacks during Troy's final two seasons at Henryetta, also remembers what a hard worker Troy was, and how he seemed to be ticketed for greatness even then.

"During the summer, I used to leave the keys to the weight room on the dash of my truck so the players could come by and lift weights if they wanted to. Troy would come over about 10:30 P.M., after he had hauled hay all day for his dad, and would leave a note on my dash that said, 'dear Coach, I borrowed your keys to go lift weights, Troy.'

"I told my daughter I was going to keep that note because it was going to be worth something one of these days."

Troy, who was a three year starter at quarterback and also played safety on defense, started showing that he was something special in his very first game, according to Monty Hall, who was the sports editor of the Henryetta Daily Free-Lance. "He threw a pass about 60 yards that turned into an 80-yard touchdown. And that touchdown won the game."

Winning games wasn't all that common at Henryetta, even when Troy was tossing the pigskin. In his three years at the helm of the Fighting Hens, the team posted records of 4-6, 2-9, and then 6-4 in Troy's senior season, which was only the fourth winning season that the school had posted over the previous 25 years. But according to Billy Holt, the former head coach of the Hens, it could have been a lot worse if Troy hadn't moved to town. "What we won, he won for us. He made lots and lots of plays for us. He was Mr. Everything at Henryetta."

Troy, who passed for 30 touchdowns and accumulated 4,764 yards of total offense in his three year career at Henryetta, was such an outstanding talent that he managed to gain all-state honors as a senior and earn honorable mention on the 1983 USA TODAY All-U.S.A. team, despite the mediocre record turned in by the Fighting Hens.

3

Kansas Twister

Despite all the ability that Troy had displayed on the football field, college recruiters didn't break down the Aikmans' door in pursuit of the All-State quarterback. And while Troy strongly considered the idea of attending college in California or at the University of Arkansas, the only schools that actively pursued *him* were Oklahoma State, which was coached by Jimmy Johnson, and the University of Oklahoma, which was coached by Barry Switzer. Although no one could have guessed it at the time, the careers of Troy and those two coaches would continue to intersect far into the future.

Troy initially leaned toward joining Johnson and his OSU Cowboys, but then he paid an official visit to OU, and decided to accept a scholarship from the Sooners, instead. "I like the town of Norman and the Oklahoma campus a lot," said Troy at the time. "After coming here and seeing the facilities, I knew I had to play here."

The decisive factor in Troy's decision, though, was Switzer's promise that the Sooners would continue to operate out of the I formation that they had been using for the past few seasons. But shortly after Troy signed his letter of intent at OU, Switzer announced that the Sooners would switch back to the wishbone offense that had been the team's trademark throughout most of Switzer's tenure at the school. The wishbone is a run-oriented, option-style, rollout offense which requires a quarterback with quick feet and not one with a strong arm.

"I wanted to go to a school where they threw the ball," said Troy, who felt trapped and betrayed by Switzer's duplicity. "I mean when I was being recruited, he told me they were going to use the 'I' and that the wishbone was obsolete, and four days after signing day they're back in the wishbone," added Troy, who also realized that his scholarship to OU might have been nothing more than Switzer's way of keeping him out of the lineup of the Sooners' cross-state rival, OSU.

Troy was also trapped and betrayed by a National Collegiate Athletic Association rule that would have forced him to sit out a season if he transferred to another school after he had signed the letter of intent. Although Troy was depressed and discouraged, he decided to make the best of a bad situation and try, somehow, to fit the round peg of his talents into the square hole of the OU offense.

Initially, because Troy was so unfamiliar with the wishbone and the Sooners seemed so well-stocked at quarterback, the coaching staff decided to redshirt Troy for his freshman season. That meant that Troy would be allowed to practice with the team and stretch his four years of college eligibility over five years, as long as he didn't play in any games during the 1984 season.

In the fourth game of the Sooners' season, though, Troy, who was still two weeks shy of his 18th birthday, was unexpectedly pressed into action against Kansas when OU's starting quarterback, senior Danny Bradley, went down with an injury and his backup was declared academically ineligible.

The Jayhawks' defenders licked their lips at the sight of a green quarterback, dug in their cleats and unleashed an unrelenting blitz against Troy. And Troy, who hadn't been properly prepared for the game by the coaching staff, turned in a wipeout of a performance. "We underestimated Kansas and overestimated what we could do," said Troy, who completed only two of 14 passes for eight yards while throwing three interceptions that were returned for a total of 90 yards and a touchdown. "We went over what we thought they were going to do, but they came out with something different and we didn't know what was going on." And OU, which had entered the game as the No. 2 ranked college team in the country, lost to the unranked Jayhawks, 28–11, their first loss to Kansas in nine years.

"That game almost ruined me as a quarterback," said Troy, who had a tough time dealing with his sense of failure. "I was crushed. I hated to go in and look at the film the next day."

Troy was also disturbed by the fact that he received very little playing time during the remainder of the 1984 season.

"It just kind of bugs me, because I know I'm a better player than a lot of people give me credit for," said Troy afterward. "As far as the Kansas game goes, things just didn't turn out. When I do bad, though, I want to get back out there and do better, and I don't really feel I had the chance to do that after the Kansas game."

4

So Long Sooners

Troy, though, was too tough to allow one game, even a devastating game like the Kansas fiasco, to place a permanent stop sign on his career. Troy even turned that negative experience into a positive one by refusing to buckle under its weight. "I think it made me grow up more as a football player," said Troy as he prepared for the 1985 season. "I've never been through an experience like that before in high school or anywhere else. I think it'll help me settle down and realize that things like that are gonna happen. You've just got to learn how to handle it."

Then Troy went out and played so well in spring practice and pre-season scrimmages that he established himself as the Sooner's No. 1 quarterback by the start of his sophomore season. "The reason he's ahead of the others is his intelligence," said Switzer. "He reads the defense, gets us in the right places and makes correct decisions. And he's also the best passer that I've ever seen in my 20 years in Norman."

While Switzer raved, Troy just shrugged. "If I was at BYU [the school where a string of quarterbacks, including Steve Young, had filled the air with footballs, and rewritten most of the NCAA passing records] I would have thought that Switzer's praise was something else. But being at Oklahoma, they've never seen anyone else throw."

Troy also realized that the picture wasn't really as bright as it seemed to be. The Sooners were still running the wishbone, and even though Switzer was prepared to let Troy throw a little, it still wasn't an offense that was suited to Troy's skills as a passer, or his lack of sprinter's speed. But Troy chose to hide his reservations and put a positive spin on the situation. "It fits me," he said. "We'll pass more, and I really like it."

Troy also refused to be cowed by the critics who still questioned his ability to run the offense, or the preseason polls which predicted a national championship for the Sooners despite the fact that they were starting a sophomore quarterback. Troy, in fact, relished the challenge.

"I think it's exciting," said Troy. "The ranking raises the expectation level of the fans. But it has the same effect on the players. We're pleased that so many people think highly of us.

"I'm not afraid of the pressure, I like pressure situations. We know we have to win every game to win the national championship. At Oklahoma, you're always expected to win. You know that coming in. Most of us came here to have the opportunity to be in just this kind of situation."

Despite Troy's firm resolve the Sooners got off to a shaky start by eeking out a 13–6 win against a very mediocre University of Minnesota squad in the 1985 season-opener. The victory was spearheaded by a supercharged defense that held the Gophers to only six first downs.

Troy, meanwhile, couldn't get the wishbone into gear, and the offense sputtered like an old jalopy with a clogged fuel line. The 13 points that OU scored was their lowest point total in a season-opener since 1966. "We didn't expect it to be so close," said Troy, who threw for a measly 647 yards while running for 34. "We expected to win big."

Troy's expectations came true the following week as the Sooners squashed a sorry Kansas State team 41–6, while rolling up 530 yards of total offense, the fourth highest total since Switzer had become head coach in 1973. Troy had the offense running like a well-oiled machine as he connected on 10 of 14 passes and added another 71 yards on the ground.

"He threw the ball real well, just like in practice," said Switzer with a smile. "He pitched some strikes even when he had defenders in his face. But he just stood in there and delivered the ball. I was real pleased with him." And Troy was real pleased to get the win, but he wasn't too thrilled about the fact that the Sooners ran the ball 76 times while attempting only 14 passes. Those weren't the types of numbers that would attract pro scouts or prepare Troy for a career in

14

the NFL.

The Sooners upped their record to 3-0 with a 14–7 taming of Texas, but once again it was the Sooners' defense that dictated the outcome of the contest. "It was the greatest defensive performance by an Oklahoma team since I've been here, and that's 20 years," said Switzer. The "D" was so dominating that the Longhorns were held to only four first downs and 17 yards rushing, the second lowest in the Longhorns' history.

The Sooners' next game turned out to be Troy's final game at OU. Ironically, Troy was having the best day of his brief career, when a jarring tackle by Miami's Jerome Brown early in the second quarter sent him to the sidelines with a broken bone in his left leg. Although OU was trailing the Jimmy Jones – coached Hurricanes 14–7, Troy had completed six of seven passes, including his first and only scoring strike as a Sooner, and had had an apparent 47-yard touchdown run called back when an official ruled that he had stepped out of bounds.

"It's a shame that Troy got hurt," said Switzer, "because he was fixin' to give the best air show ever seen around here by an Oklahoma team." Switzer also claimed that a replay showed that Troy hadn't stepped out of bounds on the TD run that was called back. "He didn't even come close to stepping on the line. Man, that was a great run. He was quick, he was fast and he made some people miss him."

While Troy was recovering from his season-ending injury, freshman Jamelle Holieway, a prototype wishbone quarterback with whippet-like speed, led the Sooners to the national championship while earning Big Eight Player of the Year honors for himself.

Although Switzer had said that the starting quarterback spot for the following season would be thrown up for grabs in spring practice, Troy didn't really need to be a weatherman to see which the wind was blowing in Norman.

"They said the job would be wide open, but I didn't think I'd have a chance, no matter how good a spring I had, after Jamelle had been the conference player of the year," said Troy. And Troy's intuition told him that Switzer would have made the change even if he hadn't broken his leg. "I think it was only a matter of time before they were going to go with Jamelle. Coach wanted to run the wishbone. No bones about it."

Switzer then confirmed Troy's analysis of the situation when he said, "We'll see Aikman in the NFL; we won't see Jamelle Holieway in the NFL. But Holieway fits our system better."

Troy decided that the best course of action for him was to tell coach Switzer that he wanted to transfer to a school that emphasized the passing game. "I wasn't happy as a football player. When we threw the ball, I felt great. The other 60 plays, I felt awkward. I wanted to go somewhere where I could throw the ball and do what I do best. And I wanted the chance to play pro ball some day."

Switzer, obligingly, picked up the telephone and called Terry Donahue, the coach of the UCLA Bruins. "If you take him," Switzer told Donahue, "he'll be a No. 1 draft choice."

5
Number One

Due to the NCAA rules on transferring, Troy was unable to play for UCLA during the 1986 season. But he was allowed to practice, and coach Donahue brought in Rick Neuheisel, a former Bruins quarterback, to tutor Troy and teach him the complex multiple offense that Donahue favored. "Where Oklahoma would have three plays designed to beat 12 defenses, UCLA has a dozen plays to counter those defenses," explained Neuheisel.

Troy, a fast learner, was quick to pick up the nuances of the Bruins' offense, and to impress Neuheisel with his outstanding potential. "There's no question he had all the tools to be a great quarterback," said Neuheisel, who had led the Bruins to the 1984 Pac-10 title and a 45–9 Rose Bowl victory over Illinois. "I like to say that he's got everything I didn't have – size, speed and a great arm. Put them all together and you have the makings of a great quarterback."

Although Donahue had given Troy a scholarship and Neuheisel had given his prized pupil high marks, Troy still had to go out and win the starting job, which he did the following spring in a duel against Brendan McCracken. Then Troy spent the summer in Los Angeles, working out with the UCLA receivers and learning their moves so that the Bruins could start the 1987 season with a bang. "All of the receivers stayed in town and worked with me, which was imperative," said Troy, "because one of the key things in throwing the football is knowing what your receivers are going to do."

Troy, who was finally playing in a system that highlighted his strength and didn't ask him to do things that didn't suit his talents, made the work pay off by leading the Bruins to a 9-2 regular-season record. The only disappointing notes in Troy's triumphant season was as 42–33 shoot down by Nebraska in the second game of the schedule, and a season-ending 17–13 loss to crosstown rival USC. The loss to USC cost the Bruins a berth in the Rose Bowl, and also cost Troy, who had thrown three interceptions, after throwing only three in the previous ten games, a couple of weeks' sleep. But Troy and his Bruins' teammates rebounded from that devastating loss with a 20–16 win over Florida in the Aloha Bowl, which upped their record to 10–2 and earned them a spot as one of the top ten college teams in the nation.

Troy's performance, which included 17 touchdown tosses, a .652 pass completion percentage and a second place finish in passing efficiency among college quarterbacks, delighted coach Donahue and also drew the praise of NFL talent scouts. "He has such great touch on his throws," said Gil Brandt, who was with the Dallas Cowboys. "He can drill the ball when he has to, but he also throws one of the most catchable balls I've ever seen anyone throw."

Troy had shown that he had the talent to throw the ball with the best of the big-time college passers, and he was thrilled to be doing it in the relatively relaxed atmosphere of cosmopolitan Los Angeles, instead of the hothouse glare of Norman, where Sooners football is the main focus for a lot of people. "At Oklahoma, you worry about what the media and fans think about you all the time," said Troy. "There's just so much emphasis on football back there. If you have a bad game, it's like you're not a good person. Here, you don't worry about what people think as much and just enjoy what you do. The expectations are there, but they aren't any higher than the expectations which I put on myself, and those are high enough."

The 1988 season looked as though it was going to be a difficult one for the Bruins, especially on offense, where only Troy and three other starters were returning from the 1987 squad. But after a season of running UCLA's multiple offense, Troy's leadership qualities flowered, and he was able to use his talent to spark the Bruins to another season among the nation's elite teams. "Knowing our offense better and what's expected of me makes it easier," said Troy. "Having that year's experience and being a year older has made me a better player."

Troy's teammate, wide receiver Mike Farr, also spoke about his improved play and leadership. "This year he's much more in his comfort zone. He's mastered our complicated offense, he knows how to read a defense a lot better, and he's a lot more mature. This year, he's like a coach on the field, and the ball is really in his hands."

With Troy at the throttle, the Bruins raced to seven straight victories, including a 41–28 payback win over Nebraska, and the top spot in the national rankings. Although the Bruins fell a few spots when they were upset by Washington State, they bounced right back with two straight wins over Pac-10 rivals and once again came into the game against USC with a Rose Bowl bid on the line. Troy and USC's quarterback, Rodney Peete, also came into the game as front-runners for the Heisman Trophy, which is given annually to the player who is selected as the best performer in college football. The media attention on Troy was so intense that coach Donahue had to limit reporters' access to him to two days per week. "Everybody in the country wants to talk to Troy. It's a wonder that the kid can even sleep."

Troy tried to minimize the effects of all the hype by downplaying the hoopla surrounding the Heisman and focusing his thoughts on the team goal of beating USC. "There's a lot of other candidates, and I don't compare my stats to theirs. If, at the end of the season, mine are good enough to win the Heisman, great. But I'd much rather beat USC and play in the Rose Bowl."

Unfortunately, Troy suffered a double disappointment. First, UCLA lost to USC, 31–22, despite a tremendous effort by Troy, who completed a school-record 32 passes while throwing for 317 yards and two touchdowns. Then Troy learned that he had finished third in the Heisman voting behind Peete, who is now, by a strange twist of fate, Troy's backup with the Cowboys, and the winner, Barry Sanders, a record-shattering running back from Oklahoma State who has gone on to become an All-Pro back with the Detroit Lions.

Troy, however, capped his collegiate career on a high note by leading the Bruins to a 17–13 win over Arkansas in the Cotton Bowl, and picking up a trophy as the game's most valuable player. In his two seasons as the Bruins' signal caller, Troy led the team to a 20–4 record, while breaking a host of school records and finishing his career as the third-rated passer in NCAA history with a passing efficiency rating of 149.7.

Troy, who was named the 1988 winner of the Davey O'Brien Award as the best college quarterback in the country, had shown that he had all the attributes of a great quarterback: accuracy (he completed .644 percent of his passes); arm strength (he threw seven scoring passes of 40 yards or more); consistency, leadership and the ability to keep drives alive with clutch third down connections (he led the Bruins on 30 TD drives of 60 yards or better while throwing for at least one touchdown in 11 of the 12 games).

Troy's pro prospects were as bright as the Hollywood sign that stands in the hills above Los Angeles. So it was no great surprise when the Dallas Cowboys selected Troy as the No. 1 pick in the 1989 NFL draft. As the first player picked, Troy knew that he was about to make some big bucks, but he wasn't about to let the money turn him inside out. "I feel fortunate to have the opportunity to make a lot of money but it won't change me. Right now, I'm totally broke. I don't have a dime on me. I'd like to help my family and I'll probably be driving a nice car and living in a nice home, but I'll still be the same."

6

Dark Days in Dallas

In 1989 the Dallas Cowboys were a team in transition. They had a new owner, Jerry Jones, and a new coach, Jimmy Johnson, former teammates at the University of Arkansas who had come to Dallas to revive a once-proud franchise that had fallen on hard times.

Johnson was brought in to replace Tom Landry, the only coach Dallas had had since it entered the league in 1960. Under Landry the Cowboys had soared to five Super Bowl appearances and 20 straight winning seasons between 1966–1985. But in the last three years of his tenure, "America's Team" had gone into a sudden tailspin, before crashing with a thud and an NFL-worst 3–13 record in 1988.

Landry's last-place finish did have a silver lining, however, because it allowed Johnson to draft the solid gold quarterback who would lead the Cowboys franchise back to its former greatness. "Troy Aikman will help restore the Cowboys' image," promised Jerry Jones at the press conference in which he introduced Troy to the media and fans in Dallas. "He's got this winning aura."

Realistically, no one expected Troy to step right in and single-handedly turn the program around. For one thing, the 1989 Cowboys' team had too many holes for any one player to plug, and for another, rookie quarterbacks rarely crack the starting lineup, let alone become pivotal factors in their teams' fortunes. As Joe Woolley, an executive with the Philadelphia Eagles put it: "Aikman's the best quarterback prospect available this year – no doubt about it. But any time you take a quarterback, you're looking at two or three years before they're really going to make an impact on your ball club. So I hope people don't expect him to come in and turn things around right away."

The reason it's so difficult for a college quarterback to step off the campus and into a starting role in the NFL has to do with how much information they have to absorb and then get comfortable with using. And the one and only way to gain that comfort is through study, practice and experience.

The inner working of quarterback play is a lot more intricate than it appears when viewed from a living room or a seat in a stadium. A quarterback first has to learn a fairly complicated code just to be able to call the proper play and the specific formation from which the play is to be run. In addition to memorizing the code and the assignments, abilities and playing habits of everyone on his own team, a quarterback also has to know the defense he's playing against well enough to be able to scan that defense at the line of scrimmage and instantaneously decide whether to go ahead with the play called in the huddle, or whether to audible into a new play because he realizes that the play called in the huddle won't work against that particular defensive alignment. Is the defense, for example, geared to stopping a running play or a passing play? Is the defensive backfield playing a zone or a man-to-man? Are they double-covering a receiver? But perhaps the main question that the quarterback better know the answer to is: Are one or more of those very nasty-looking, very agile 250-pound linebackers about to come blitzing across the line of scrimmage to try and sack the QB? And since the quarterback has to read the defense and make his decision in just a few seconds, he has to know the formations and assignments so well that he can do all that as automatically as he would cross a street when the light turns green.

John Hadl, a former coach and Hall of Fame signal caller, knows exactly what it's like to be a rookie quarterback and see the players moving without being able to decipher the patterns. "Things happen so fast out there, it's like a jail break. You're getting coached a lot. You have to learn the system and the way your coaches want it done. Then you start to think quite a bit, and sometimes you think too much. Then you go blank."

John Elway, who is widely considered to be the greatest college quarterback to ever play the game, also remembers the rough times that he had in his rookie year with the Denver Broncos. After starting the first five games of the season, Elway was benched and thoroughly bewildered. "I was so confused. My mind was going a hundred miles a minute, and with all that static in my brain, I couldn't react. I worried about calling the formations and getting the play off without getting hit with a delay of game penalty. I couldn't even *think* about the defense."

A further complicating factor for Troy was the fact that the Cowboys' coaching staff, in a gallant effort to rebuild a last-place team, were continually shuffling players on and off the roster. Being a rookie quarterback is a harsh enough sentence, but being a rookie quarterback on a terrible team that is also in constant chaos, is cruel and unusual punishment. "Sometimes you'd get in the huddle and be meeting a teammate for the first time," recalled linebacker Ken Norton, one of the few survivors from those dark days in Dallas.

Those moves would eventually pay big dividends, especially the blockbuster October trade that sent Herschel Walker, the Cowboys' only Pro-Bowl player, to the Minnesota Vikings in exchange for a package of players and future draft picks that would provide the essential underpinnings for the current team. But in the short term, the team and Troy suffered. "We were bringing in new guys every week," recalled Troy, who beat out veteran Babe Laufenberg and fellow rookie Steve Walsh for the starting quarterback role. "We couldn't get any better because we spent most of the time just teaching the new guys what we were doing."

Despite the turmoil and the confusion and the holes where there were supposed to be blockers, Troy was fulfilling a boyhood dream when he trotted on the field for the opening game of the 1989 season. But the New Orleans Saints quickly turned the game into a nightmare for Troy as they sacked him twice, picked off two of his passes and shut out the Cowboys 28–0. The following week, in Atlanta, Troy threw his first NFL touchdown pass, a 65-yard strike to Michael Irvin that would prove to be an omen of better days to come, but the Falcons also picked off two more of his passes and sent the Cowboys to their second straight defeat.

The next two contests introduced Troy to the rough-and-tumble world of the NFC East as a pair of divisional rivals invaded Texas Stadium. First, Washington came to town and made Troy's first home game a less than memorable experience: they picked off a pair of passes, sacked him four times and held him to six completions in 21 attempts for only 83 yards. Then the Giants rode into Dallas and allowed Troy to complete one pass before they drove him into the ground and sent him off the field with a broken left index finger that kept him on the sidelines for the following five weeks.

As Troy sat and watched, the Cowboys dropped four more games and posted their only win of the season, 13–3 over Washington. Then Troy returned to action against the Phoenix Cardinals and showed everyone why he had been the No. 1 pick in the draft, as he threw for an NFL-rookie record 379 yards and two touchdowns, including an 80-yard dazzler that gave Dallas a 20–17 lead with only 1:43 left to play. Troy, though, paid the price for the pass as soon as he released it by being hammered headfirst into the ground and knocked unconscious. And while Troy was sitting on the sidelines being revived by smelling salts, the Cards came right back and posted the points that sent the Cowboys to another torturous defeat. "That was probably as low as I've ever been," said Troy. "I knew it couldn't get any worse."

But it sure didn't get much better anytime soon either. Although Troy completed a season-high 25 passes the following week against the Miami Dolphins, Dallas dropped another close game, and then the Philadelphia Eagles, the Cowboys' most intense rivals, swooped down on Texas Stadium and shut out the Cowboys 27–0 while picking off three of Troy's throws and limiting him to 54 yards on 7 of 21 passing.

Although battered, Troy refused to flinch and the following week he hit for four TD tosses against the LA Rams. But that was the last highlight of the year for Troy, before the final trio of games turned into a "Lowlights-of-the-Season" feature, starting with the Eagles sinking their talons into Troy and sacking him a season-high five times. The Giants kept the reel going by handing the Cowboys their third shutout of the year, and then Troy threw a career-high four interceptions in the season finale against the Green Bay Packers.

Troy had been battered and knocked out and had broken a bone, but his spirit, although dented, remained unbowed, despite Dallas' dismal and NFL-worst 1-15 record. There had certainly been a lot more low points than high points but Troy, who was named to most of the All-Rookie teams, had shown that he had the talent and the toughness to see better days and do better things. And Troy's outlook was also brightened by reading the biography of TV analyst Terry Bradshaw, a former No. 1 draft pick who had stumbled for a few seasons before going on to quarterback the Pittsburgh Steelers to four Super Bowls and earn entry into the NFL Hall of Fame. "It was helpful to learn that my situation wasn't unique and that other players had also gone through some rough times," said Troy. "I realized that everyone has their trials and tribulations and if you just keep battling, it will come out all right."

7

Giant Steps

The Cowboys took a giant step toward the development of a championship caliber team in 1990 when they drafted running back Emmitt Smith and signed free agent tight end Jay Novacek. Smith, the first dividend from the Herschel Walker trade, went on to rush for over 900 yards and be named the NFC Offensive Rookie of the Year, while Novacek, after five mediocre seasons with the Cardinals, developed into one of the top tight ends in the NFL.

The improved play of young veterans such as fullback Daryl Johnston, center Mark Stepnoski, defensive end Tony Tolbert and linebacker Ken Norton, was another key element in the Cowboys' rise to a 7-9 record. But no one played a larger role in the team's turnaround than Troy, who put the winning points on the scoreboard in the fourth quarter in six of the Cowboys' seven wins.

Troy got the Cowboys off to a quick start by scoring his first NFL touchdown with only 1:58 left on the clock to lift the team to a 17–14 opening-day victory against the San Diego Chargers. After that promising win, though, the Cowboys went into a three-game stall with a pair of lopsided losses to the Giants sandwiched around a 19–15 loss at Washington in which Troy suffered 8 sacks.

The team was in a skid and in danger of careening out of control the following week when they trailed the Tampa Bay Buccaneers 10–7 late in the fourth quarter. But Troy stepped up and engineered a game-winning 80-yard drive that he capped with a 28-yard scoring strike to Michael Irvin, who was back in action for the first time since ripping up his knee in the sixth game of the 1989 season.

The Cowboys then hit another icy patch on their road to respectability, and dropped four of their next five games, including a 24–6 scalding by the San Francisco 49ers in which Troy was sacked twice, picked off once and held to only 96 yards passing. But just as the team was on the verge of sliding off the slope, Troy got them back on track by tossing three TD passes and leading them on an 89-yard fourth-quarter drive that positioned the field goal which gave them a last-gasp 24–21 win over the Los Angeles Rams.

Four days later, in a nationally televised Thanksgiving Day game, Troy kept the Cowboys' engine humming with two long fourth-quarter drives that propelled Dallas to a 27–17 win over Washington. Troy put on a carbon copy performance the following week, as he connected on 11 straight second-half passes while directing two more fourth-quarter scoring drives that catapulted the Cowboys to a 17–13 comeback victory over the Saints.

The Cowboys continued on their merry way with a 41–10 clobbering of the Cardinals that gave the franchise its first four-game winning streak since 1985 and evened their record at 7-7. With two games left on their schedule, the Cowboys needed only one more win to put themselves into the playoff picture. But it never happened.

After Troy had thrown his only pass of the day, he was driven to the ground by a hard hit from Eagles end Clyde Simmons and wound up needing season-ending surgery on his right shoulder. With Troy on the sidelines, the Cowboys' offense sputtered to a stop and so did their dream of a place in the playoffs.

During his first two seasons in the league, Troy's report card was a mixed bag. He had been picked off 36 times while throwing only 20 TD passes, and his QB rating was somewhere south of ugly. But Troy had completed more than 55 percent of his passes, and had shown that he had the toughness to stand and deliver despite absorbing 58 sacks, countless knockdowns and two serious injuries. Troy had also demonstrated the rare ability to rally his team and put the winning points on the scoreboard late in the game. In the six fourth-quarter rallies that Troy had sparked, he completed a spectacular 71.1 percent of his passes, for 456 yards, two TD's and no interceptions. That capacity to stay cool and raise the level of your play when the game is on the line is, more than anything, what separates the superstar from the rest of the pack.

The pluck that Troy had shown in standing in the pocket and taking his hits plus the coolness that he had shown in pulling out late-game wins earned him a spot on the All-Madden Team selected by football's top television analyst, John Madden.

The Cowboys took some more giant steps toward a championship in 1991, starting with the hiring of offensive coordinator Norv Turner, who had an immediate and positive effect on Troy's continuing development. "We hit it off from day one," said Troy. "I felt very strongly about his offensive system." Next, the Cowboys had another dynamite draft that corralled wide receiver Alvin Harper and an awesome array of defensive talent, including tackles Russell Maryland and Leon Lett and linebackers Dixon Edwards and Larry Brown. Finally, the Cowboys picked the pockets of the Falcons, when they snared veteran defensive tackle Tony Casillas for a pair of 1992 draft choices.

Troy, for one, was looking at the upcoming season with a lot of optimism. "It's exciting to think of where we've come in the two years I've been here, and I think there's a great future coming."

Then Troy went out and started creating that bright new future by throwing five TD passes in the first two games of the season and throwing 93 straight passes without an interception. After the Eagles dimmed the lights by picking off three passes and shutting out the Cowboys, Troy turned on the high beams and led Dallas on a four-game winning streak, which included a 21–16 triumph over the Giants for which Troy was named the NFC Offensive Player of the Week after he capped an 84-yard drive with a game-winning TD pass to Michael Irvin.

Although Troy was enjoying the best year of his brief career, he couldn't prevent the Cowboys from falling into a midseason slump in which they lost three of four games and saw their record drop to 6-5. Troy, though, was riding high, leading the NFC in completions and passing yardage, as the Cowboys came into Washington looking for a win that would keep their playoff hopes on track. Troy did his part by passing for over 300 yards and leading the Cowboys to a 14–7 advantage before he was knocked out of the game with a sprained knee midway through the third quarter. Backup Steve Beuerlein, an offseason pickup from the Los Angeles Raiders, finished off the 24–21 win over Washington and then went on to lead the Cowboys to four straight season-ending victories that upped their record to 11-5 and secured their place in the playoffs. As Troy watched from the sidelines, Beuerlein was brilliant in the stretch run, connecting on a TD pass in each of the five games in which he played, while throwing 111 consecutive passes without an interception, the sixth longest streak in franchise history. Beuerlein continued his touchdown throwing streak as the Cowboys beat the Bears 17–13, in a wild-card playoff game at Soldier Field in Chicago. The bubble finally burst for Beuerlein and the Cowboys the following week when they were destroyed by the Detroit Lions, 38–6, in a divisional playoff game.

Troy had once again ended the season on a disappointing note. Although he was happy that Dallas had made it into the playoffs, he was frustrated at not being able to be a part of the stretch drive or the playoff action, except for some unwanted mop-up duty against the Lions. But Troy, who led the NFC in pass completion percentage and earned his first trip to the Pro Bowl, adopted a positive point of view. "We accomplished a lot of great things. I think everybody can hold their heads up high and be really excited about going into next season."

8

The Big Breakthrough

After three seasons in the NFL, Troy had proved that he was a highly accurate passer who was even capable of occasional flashes of brilliance, but he still hadn't established himself as one of the league's elite quarterbacks. He had, though, like the team as a whole, shown steady improvement, and 1992 looked like it just might be the year that Troy was ready to have a breakthrough season and lead the Cowboys to the Big Jackpot.

Troy and his teammates showed they were for real by winning eight of their first nine games, including a Monday Night opening game against Washington, the defending Super Bowl champions. The Cowboys kept on rolling with victories over the Giants and the Cardinals as Troy connected on five touchdown passes without throwing a single interception. Then came a bump in the road as the Cowboys traveled to Philadelphia, where they were flattened by their old nemesis, 31–7, while Troy was picked off three times.

The Cowboys then tore off on a five-game unbeaten streak, which included a payback win over the Eagles and another against Detroit, when they demolished the Lions, 37–3. After a close loss to the LA Rams, the Cowboys strung together a trio of wins starting with a game in Phoenix in which Troy completed a season-high 25 passes and threw for a pair of touchdowns, and ending in a 31–27 thriller over the Broncos in which Troy connected on three TD tosses, and completed 7-of-8 passes for 78 yards on a last-minute, game-winning touchdown drive in Denver.

After a road loss to Washington in which Troy reached 10,000 passing yards in his 52nd game, faster than any QB in team history, the Cowboys closed out their season by coasting to a pair of easy wins that raised their record to 13-3, tops in the NFC East.

The Cowboys' climb to the top of the divisional standings had been fueled by a total team effort. The defense, which had been strengthened by the addition of pass-rushing specialist Charles Haley and a trio of rookie starters, was lightning quick and finished the season as the top-rated unit in the NFL. And offensively the Cowboys, who were the second highest scoring team in the NFL, simply had too many weapons for other teams to neutralize. Emmitt Smith had won his second consecutive rushing title behind a line that featured a pair of Pro Bowl players, center Mark Stepnoski and guard Nate Newton. And both tight end Jay Novacek and wide receiver Michael "The Playmaker" Irvin had been named to their second straight Pro Bowl squad.

But if there was a key ingredient in the Cowboys' spectacular success story, it was the emergence of Troy Aikman as one of the league's top signal callers. "He's one player who took it to another level this year," declared Dallas owner Jerry Jones. And the best was yet to come.

Troy made his first playoff start a memorable one by playing with the precision of a skilled surgeon and leading the Cowboys to an unexpectedly easy 34–10 win over the Eagles. Troy, who threw for two hundred yards and a pair of first-half touchdowns, was named the NFL Post Season Player of the Week.

The win over the Eagles sent the Cowboys to San Francisco for an NFC Championship game showdown against the 49ers, the owners of the league's best record, 14–2, and highest-scoring offense. At the controls of that high-flying offense was southpaw Steve Young, the league's top-rated passer and the NFL's MVP for 1992.

The game appeared to be a tossup between two high-powered, evenly matched teams, and the 10–10 halftime score didn't do anything to dispel that idea. But on the first series of the third quarter, Troy lifted the level of his play and led the Cowboys on a long scoring drive that put them in the lead 17–10. Then in the fourth quarter, Troy capped another long drive by beating a pair of blitzing linebackers with a pass to Emmitt Smith on a third-and-goal from the 49ers' 16-yard line. "He never flinched," said offensive tackle Mark Tuinei. "Every time we needed a big play on third down, he got it for us."

Perhaps the biggest play in a day of big plays occurred right after the 49ers had closed the gap 24–20. Instead of trying to work the clock and sit on their small lead the Cowboys went for the clincher. "That's been our style ever since I've been here," said Troy. "Always go for it, always attack, no matter what the score is." Troy made the strategy work by hitting Alvin Harper on a 70-yard catch-and-run play down to the 49ers' nine-yard line, and then delivering a scoring dart to Kelvin Martin that made the final score 30–20 and earned Troy his second consecutive Post Season Player of the Week Award. "Troy played the game as well as it can be played," said Norv Turner, Dallas' offensive coordinator. "He'll have more games like this, but you have to appreciate this one."

Two weeks later Troy capped his breakthrough season with a breathtaking display of football brilliance that carried the Cowboys to a 52–17 blowout of the Buffalo Bills in Super Bowl XXVII. Ironically, Troy got off to a slow start as a combination of big-game jitters and a tough two-deep, blitzing defense temporarily stymied him. "I was having a tough time getting into the feeling of the game," acknowledged Troy. "I really had to talk myself into relaxing."

Some sideline advice from Norv Turner midway through the first quarter helped Troy to settle down. "I told Troy, 'If they take away the deep routes, go underneath.' " And that's exactly what Troy did on the Cowboys' next possession, which he capped with a 23-yard TD pass to Jay Novacek. "That was a heck of a throw," said Turner. "All Troy needed was a little direction and a feeling for something that would work. He's never had an ounce of doubt about his ability. You wouldn't make the throws he makes unless you have unbelievable confidence."

In the second quarter Troy quickly teamed up with Michael Irvin on a pair of TD passes that gave the Cowboys a 28–10 halftime lead and began to turn the game into the biggest rout in Super Bowl history. "I settled down in the second quarter and got on a roll," explained Troy, who wound up throwing four touchdown passes and becoming the youngest quarterback since Joe Montana to be named the Super Bowl MVP. "When I get like that, I feel I can take control of a game and complete every pass I throw. Once I got into that groove, I knew there was no way they were going to stop us." As the last seconds of the game ticked off the clock, Troy, who had thrown eight TD passes without an interception in the three postseason games while setting an all-time record with a 116.7 QB rating, was flooded with a rush of thoughts and feelings. He thought back to his rookie year and all the doubts that had haunted him. "We all had some doubts. At that stage, when you're 1-15, it's hard to see the light at the end of the tunnel." Troy also explained the great relief that he felt as the game ended. "Winning this game meant everything to me. It's a tremendous weight off my shoulders. No matter what happens from here on out, I took a team to the Super Bowl and won.

"But now that I've won one," said Troy, looking to the future, "I don't want to be greedy but I'd like to win another one. I'll enjoy this time as much as the next guy, but I won't do anything that will take away from my preparation for training camp and next season."

In May, though, while Troy was working out at the team's Valley Ranch training center, he suddenly suffered a severe case of back spasms. Three weeks later, Troy was having surgery on a herniated disc that would sideline him until the final two games of the season.

With Troy still not sharp and Emmitt Smith sitting out in a contract dispute, the out-of-sync Cowboys' offense sputtered and the defending Super Bowl champions dropped the first two games of the 1993 season.

By the time the team traveled to Phoenix for their third game, Smith had signed his contract and Troy was as hot as the flame at the end of a welder's torch. "Aikman was magnificent," raved Fritz Shurmur, the Cardinals' defensive coordinator. "It was the best I've seen a quarterback throw the ball. Every receiver he hit was on the run and the ball was right there. He's definitely one of the top two quarterbacks in the league."

The win over the Cardinals sparked the Cowboys to a seven-game winning streak, which included a 26–17 win over the 49ers and a 23–10 win over the Eagles in which Emmitt Smith galloped through the mud for 237 yards, the sixth best single-game rushing performance in NFL history.

The Cowboys' string was finally snapped by Atlanta as Troy sat on the sideline with an ankle injury. The Cowboys also lost their next game, 16–14, when a last-second blunder by Leon Lett allowed Dolphins' kicker Pete Stoyanovich to boot a game-winning field goal. But then the team put together a season-ending five-game winning streak capped by a crucial 16–13 overtime win against the Giants.

The Cowboys' win against the Giants, which carried Dallas to their second consecutive NFC Eastern Division title and an NFC-best 12-4 record, also paved their way into postseason play. Troy kept the momentum running in high gear by passing for 302 yards and three TD's as the Cowboys beat the Green Bay Packers in a divisional playoff game, 27–17. Jimmy Johnson was so giddy at the way the team was playing that he phoned a Dallas call-in show and "guaranteed" a Cowboy win over the 49ers in the upcoming NFC championship game. Then Troy went out and backed up Johnson's words by leading the Cowboys to touchdowns on four of their first five possessions. The only time the Cowboys didn't click was when Alvin Harper dropped Troy's 39-yard end-zone lob. "They just went up and down the field on us," said a dazzled Tim McDonald, the 49ers' All-Pro safety. Two plays into the third quarter, with Dallas holding on to a 28–7 lead in a game that they would win 38–21, Troy was knocked unconscious by a knee inadvertently cracking into his helmet. The team doctor knew that Troy's day was done when he couldn't remember who had won Super Bowl XXVII, or who had been the game's MVP. And when the doctor asked where Super Bowl XXVIII was going to be played, Troy said, "Henryetta."

Although Troy did spend a few scary nights in a hospital, he recovered in time to quarterback the Cowboys to their second consecutive Super Bowl win and send the Bills to their fourth straight Super Bowl loss, 30–13.

The Cowboys had become only the fifth team to win back-to-back Super Bowls, and Troy was too busy basking in the satisfaction of the moment to want to think ahead about their prospects of becoming the only NFL team to "Three-peat."

"It's too early to call us the Team of the Nineties. But I guess this says last year wasn't a fluke. It puts us with some great teams. What exactly that means to all of us, I'm not sure."

9

Looking Ahead

If Troy was looking ahead to a relaxing offseason, he was in for a big surprise. Even before the glow of the team's second Super Bowl had begun to dim, it seemed that the Cowboys' theme song had become, "They're breaking up that old gang of mine."

First, Norv Turner left to accept the head coaching job with Washington, and some key players, including Tony Casillas and Ken Norton, went to other teams as free agents. Then Jerry Jones shocked just about everyone when he fired Jimmy Johnson and replaced him with Barry Switzer, the former coach of the Oklahoma Sooners. Jones, though, first made sure that Troy, the QB he had recently signed to an 8-year, $50 million contract, the richest in NFL history, would support Switzer. And Troy's support was so crucial that Switzer also met with him, even before he attended the press conference announcing his appointment as the third coach in the history of the franchise. "The first guy I had to meet with was Troy because of what he represents to this team," said Switzer, who had been out of coaching for the last five years. "Not only because he's the best quarterback in the universe, but because he has such a great feel for the football team and has earned the respect of his teammates."

Troy, who had long ago patched up his problem with Switzer, didn't hide his disappointment concerning Johnson's departure, but he also set the tone for the rest of the team by his praise of Switzer. "Of all the coaches I've had, he's without question the best motivator I've been around. He does a great job of communicating at a player's level."

Troy, as a team leader, also took it upon himself to do what he could to make sure that his teammates stayed with the program and focused on the future. "We have to prepare for the upcoming season and get ready to compete. I'm still confidant that we can keep this going in the right direction and win another Super Bowl," said Troy, who holds the NFL's career postseason records for completion percentage and QB rating.

Troy, who is a somewhat shy and self-contained person, has never been a rah-rah type of in-your-face leader. He's always preferred to lead quietly and by example, but there's never been any reason to doubt his effectiveness. Bill Bates, the veteran safety with the Cowboys, points out that no one but Troy speaks in the team's huddle. "That says something. If Troy can get that kind of respect from Michael Irvin and Emmitt Smith, you know right away that it's his team."

When Troy's away from the field he likes to spend a lot of time with a couple of friends from UCLA who now live in Dallas. Troy usually prefers relaxing in private with his friends to going out in public where he usually becomes the center of attention, an attention that he finds puzzling. "The thing about me is I don't feel I'm different from anybody else just because I happen to be the quarterback of the Dallas Cowboys," said Troy.

Although football occupies most of Troy's time, even in the off-season when he still works out on a regular basis, he also expends a lot of time and money helping others. Troy has helped raise money for more than a dozen organizations, including the United Way, the Special Olympics and Stars For Children. Troy cares so much about helping children that in 1992 he started the Troy Aikman Foundation especially to provide money for needy children.

"There is a kid out there who might need $10,000 for a surgery, or who needs $20,000 to get on a donor list. The reason what we're doing is unique is we'll be able to directly touch that child. We'll be able to directly help that child.

"I had a pretty good childhood," Aikman continued. "When I started visiting hospitals when I was in college, I began to understand how many kids are out there who aren't so fortunate.

"It is my belief that childhood should be a wondrous time of life, a time of dreaming, discovery, development and play. There is nothing more important than the health and well-being of children in our nation."

Troy has also given a lot back to the people of Henryetta. He has established two annual scholarships that provide money for high school graduates to use toward their college educations, and he also donated $20,000 to help build a new sports center for the town. "The place is still a part of me," explained Troy at the center's dedication. And the people of Henryetta, who had already named two streets after Troy, showed how they felt when they voted to call the new facility the Troy Aikman Sports Center. "He was a class act as a kid growing up here," said Henryetta's mayor, Tom Henry. "And he's a class act now as a fine young man."

1. Running the wishbone.
Courtesy of the University of Oklahoma

College Football's Top Gun

UCLA Quarterback Troy Aikman
Heisman Trophy Candidate

2. About to strike
Courtesy of UCLA

3. Troy buys some time
Courtesy of Bill Hickey/ ALLSPORT USA

4. Blowing away the Bills
Courtesy of Rick Stewart ALLSPORT USA Super Bowl XXVII

5. Taking it to the 49ers.
Courtesy of Don Smith SPORTS PHOTO MASTERS, INC.

6. Steve sets up at BYU
Courtesy of BYU

7. I'm out of here
Courtesy of Don Smith SPORTS PHOTO MASTERS, INC.

8. This one's for you Jerry.
Courtesy of Otto Greule Jr. ALL-SPORT USA

9. It's time to run.
Courtesy of Otto Greule Jr. ALL-SPORT USA

10. Picture Perfect.
Courtesy of Jim Commentucci ALL-SPORT USA

STEVE YOUNG

1

Getting it Right

Jon Steven Young was born October 11, 1961, in Salt Lake City, Utah, and lived there until his family moved to the posh suburb of Greenwich, Connecticut, when he was six years old.

Steve showed that he had unusual strength and athleticism when he was still just a toddler. "He was particularly well coordinated," recalled his dad, LeGrande, who is called Grit by almost everyone, including his wife, Sherry. "One day while I was doing push-ups, Steve, who was only two and one half years old, asked if he could try. I said sure and he got down and did ten of them. By the time he was three, he was dribbling a basketball and getting it right," added Steve's dad who, in 1959, before he was a corporate lawyer, set the single-season rushing record at Brigham Young University.

In fact, the entire Young family – which includes Steve's younger sister and three younger brothers – is filled with outstanding athletes. Their home life was so centered around athletic events that when Sherry Young was asked about how the family spent its time, she replied, "Mostly we go to games."

But life wasn't only fun and games for Steve. When he was nine years old he was regularly beaten up by a schoolyard bully, and he was always the last boy taken in the neighborhood football games. "Those were some of the toughest days of my life," recalled Steve.

Steve also had to learn another of life's hard lessons, that losing is just as much a part of playing as winning. "He was a sore loser as a kid," said Steve's mom. "If he lost, you couldn't talk to him for a day. He always blamed himself."

When Steve was nine, he also got to go to his first ball camp, where he met Mike Ornato. Ornato was the coach of the Greenwich High School Football team, and he made an extra-large impression on Steve. "In my mind, there was the president of the United States, my father and the high school coach." Right then Steve started dreaming that one day he would start playing football at Greenwich High.

Although Steve's dad had been a football player, he never pushed Steve to follow in his footsteps. "My dad always told me not to play football if it wasn't fun. That's the most important part when you're young. But he also told me to give it all I had once I had decided to do it."

Steve had absolutely no trouble deciding that he wanted to play football, but he did give a lot of thought to whether or not he wanted to practice the Mormon religion, as his parents did. "I had to decide early on what I believed in because I was living something that was hard to live," said Steve, referring to the Mormon strictures against cursing, smoking and drinking. Steve decided to join the church, even though it meant that he'd be behaving differently than all of his friends. "Growing up in Connecticut, I used to think there were only four Mormons in the world – my parents, me and Brigham Young," said Steve, in a smiling reference to the founder of the religion and Steve's great-great-great-grandfather.

In high school, when Steve went out to parties with his friends, some of them would drink beer, but Steve always drank milk. "But my friends always respected me, and no human being ever had more fun," said Steve, who always acted as the designated driver.

Steve was also a straight-A student in the classroom as well as a three-sport star on the playing field. His talent and personality commanded so much respect from his teammates and his coaches at Greenwich High that he was elected captain of the baseball, basketball and football teams. In his senior year Steve, who throws left-handed but bats right-handed, was the school's top pitcher and a .600 hitter on the diamond, a 20-points-per-game scorer on the basketball court, and an All-County quarterback who led an undermanned team to the district championship game.

"He took a team of very average athletes to that game," said coach Ornato. "He was a tremendous athlete and he always had a great work ethic, too." The one thing that Steve didn't have was a strong arm. "He was an excellent runner, but he wasn't gifted with a naturally strong arm," added Ornato. "As a sophomore and junior, in fact, he had a less than average arm for a high school quarterback."

Of course, playing in the run-oriented wishbone offense that Ornato coached wasn't the type of system designed to help a quarterback develop his arm. "I don't think we ever practiced throwing the ball in high school," said Steve. "We threw maybe 10 times a game. I was actually embarrassed to throw the ball in public. I didn't enjoy throwing because I wasn't very good at it. We had to throw out of a rollout, no dropbacks. That's hard to do even now. I always just ran the ball. Why embarrass yourself?"

Steve's lack of experience in passing a football became a problem when it was time to decide on a college. Although Steve's grades would have gained him admission to just about any school in the country, Steve wanted to attend a school that had a strong football program as well as academic opportunities.

But weak-armed quarterbacks don't tend to set the hearts of college recruiters beating strongly. In fact, the only college that actively recruited Steve was North Carolina, and they didn't plan on playing him at quarterback. "Above all, we thought he was an outstanding athlete," said Jack Himebauch, who was UNC's recruiting director. "We recruited him as a quarterback, but we thought he'd end up as a running back. They were a wishbone team and Steve liked to call his own number. When he turned upfield, he usually made something good happen."

In the meantime, Steve got to meet LaVell Edwards, the head coach of Brigham Young University, when Edwards came east to give a talk. Steve must have done some pretty fancy talking himself, because Edwards invited him to come out to BYU for a recruiting visit. But the trip turned into a disappointment when an assistant coach told him, "The only chance you have of playing here is by becoming a defensive back."

2

Cougar Country

That warning almost pushed Steve into accepting the scholarship offer from UNC, but in the end he decided on BYU instead. "It had nothing to do with my family ties there. I mean, who really thinks about their great-great-great-grandfather?" said Steve, referring to Brigham Young. "And I wasn't around when my father played there. It was just a gut feeling that it would be the right place for me."

It must have seemed like a strange choice to everyone else, though, since Steve had never impressed anyone with his throwing ability and coach Edwards had installed an offensive system that was so heavily geared toward the passing game, that their initials could have been AIR BYU.

Since Edwards' arrival at the school in 1972 he had turned out a trio of topflight quarterbacks, all of whom had finished their college careers among the top ten rated passers in NCAA history. But the fourth in the Edwards assembly line and the best of the bunch was Jim McMahon, who would end his career as the No. 1 rated college QB of all time.

When Steve arrived on the field for his first practice in the fall of 1980, he was listed as the team's eighth-string QB, the very end of a long line that stretched up to McMahon, who was in his junior year. The first thing that Steve did was walk up and introduce himself to quarterback coach Dick Scovil, who was conducting a passing drill with the other QB's on the team. The second thing that Steve did was take a snap from the center, drop back and then trip over his own feet and fall right down on his backside. "Everyone laughed. I was so embarrassed."

Since the coaching staff didn't have any time to waste on an eighth-stringer, Steve worked on his own and learned whatever he could from watching McMahon.

"I tried to pick up as much on my own as I could. Just the way

McMahon would practice taking snaps without a center. When I did it, I would cheat a little and place my fingers in exactly the right grip on the ball so I wouldn't have to adjust it while I was dropping back. But I noticed that Jim didn't do that. He shifted the ball from his left hand to his right while he dropped back, just like he would have to do in a game. I thought, 'Why am I cheating myself?' After that I practiced better."

Nonetheless, in December, at the end of Steve's first season, he still hadn't climbed up the depth chart, so coach Edwards, acting on the advice of QB coach Scovil, told Steve that he wasn't a part of BYU's plans as a quarterback. "I think we have our quarterbacks for the future," said Edwards. "We need defensive backs. We'd like to move you to safety. You're too good an athlete to sit around."

The news hit Steve so hard that he called his parents and told them that he was dropping out of college and coming home. "But my dad told me that if I left school I couldn't live at home. 'There are no quitters living here,' Dad told me, and that settled that.

"Looking back. I think almost every freshman goes through a shock like I did. You go from being the big high school star to eighth-string, and it's a big disappointment. I just needed someone to tell me to keep going."

One month later Steve's football career and, most likely, his entire life changed direction when coach Scovil resigned and was replaced by a new QB coach, Ted Tollner. During his first day on the job Tollner watched the quarterbacks throwing, and then told Edwards that he thought Steve had the tools to become the team's future quarterback. Edwards checked out Steve the next day and came to the same exact conclusion.

"He was an eye-catcher with his foot speed and his quick release," recalled Tollner. "The only thing that did not grade at the top was his arm. He had *good* velocity, but not *great* velocity."

Tollner had given Steve the chance that he had been hoping for and working toward. "All I wanted was a shot. With Scovil, I wasn't even getting a look. I thought I could throw. I just wanted a chance to do it. If I didn't make it after that, I would have played defensive back, receiver, running back, wherever they needed me."

By the time Steve's sophomore season was set to start, he had leapfrogged up the depth chart to No. 2, right behind McMahon. And when McMahon went down with a knee injury in the middle of the 1981 season, Steve stepped in and threw for over 300 yards while leading the Cougars to a 32–26 win over Western Athletic Conference – rival Utah State. Steve, the first southpaw QB in BYU history, was back at the controls the following week, but this time his 21 completions weren't enough to stop the Cougars from a loss that ended their 17-game winning streak.

McMahon was back in action for the next game, and he played so well that he finished third in the voting for the Heisman Trophy. But during his brief stint, Steve had shown that the string of super quarterbacks at BYU would remain unbroken, the torch had been passed.

But when Steve stepped into the starter's role in the fall of 1982, he also stepped into a bright spotlight. Following in the footsteps of McMahon and the other Cougar quarterback stars created a lot of expectations, and after the first few games there was some doubt as to whether Steve could deliver the goods. The second game of his junior season, in particular, turned into a nightmare when the Georgia Bulldogs picked off *six* of Steve's passes. The following week, in a game that marked the inauguration of the expansion of BYU's stadium from a 35,000-person capacity to 66,000, the Cougars lost to the Air Force, one of BYU's WAC rivals.

The back-to-back losses stung Steve and shook his confidence. "There were times that I questioned myself in those early days," acknowledged Steve. "But I convinced myself that a throwing football team will make mistakes, and that I had to keep plugging away."

Which is exactly what Steve did. And his positive thinking helped him steady down and lead the Cougars to seven straight conference wins, which earned them the WAC championship and an invitation to play Ohio State in the Holiday Bowl. And while the Buckeyes put a damper on BYU's festivities by putting an emphatic, 47–17, end to the Cougars' winning streak, Steve still managed to throw for over 300 yards and wind up with 3,507 yards of total offense, the second highest in the nation for 1982 and the third highest single-season total in BYU history.

The total numbers showed 3,100 yards passing, including an NCAA record 22 straight pass completions over a two-game stretch, a 62.7 completion percentage and 18 scoring passes, as well as 407 yards and another 10 touchdowns rushing. That performance earned Steve WAC Offensive Player of the Year honors and the ringing endorsement of Gil Brandt, who was the top talent scout of the Dallas Cowboys. "He's the best they've ever had there. And he's the most accurate passer I've *ever* seen. Period. Young simply refuses to throw a bad pass."

Steve, however, was far from satisfied with his performance. "If I complete 20 of 23 passes, I remember the three," said Steve, a perfectionist by nature, and someone who, perhaps, dwells too much on the misses and doesn't take enough satisfaction from the hits.

As he was about to start his senior season, Steve also acknowledged, for the first time, just how burdened he had felt by picking up the QB reins at BYU. "I tried to tell people that there wasn't a lot of extra pressure on me, but let's face it, there obviously was. It's hard to go out there and play your best when you're constantly thinking about trying to be as good as the ones who had played there before you. I think I'll be a lot more comfortable this year."

Although it seemed unlikely that Steve could play at a higher level than he had achieved in the previous season, that's precisely what he did. Steve kicked off the 1983 schedule by passing for 351 yards and a single TD, while picking up another pair of scores and 113 yards on the ground. And even though the Cougars wound up on the short end of a 40–36 shoot-out, Baylor coach Grant Teaff had caught enough of Steve. "I rate Young as the best quarterback I've seen. He does it all. We just couldn't contain him. He's faster than a lot of halfbacks."

After that opening game loss, Steve led the Cougars to 11 straight wins, and continued to light up the scoreboard while picking up yardage at a record-setting pace. Over the course of the next three games Steve bombarded Bowling Green with five touchdown passes and two TD runs; threw for two scores and completed an NCAA-record 18 straight passes against the Air Force; and threw for another pair of scores in leading BYU over UCLA, 37–35.

The Bruins were so intent on stopping Steve's passing that they played seven men deep, allowing the BYU running game to ramble for 265 yards. "Young is the closest player we've seen since John Elway to being a great quarterback," said UCLA coach Terry Donahue.

What helped to make Steve so outstanding was his enthusiasm for the game and his willingness to constantly work at improving his skills. "I love practice. I can't wait to go back out each day. It never gets monotonous. It's a constant challenge," said Steve. "I haven't got to the point where I think I'm pretty good and I don't have to work anymore. This game is fun and I intend to keep it that way. And as long as I work hard, I think my play will continue to improve."

Toward the end of Steve's spectacular senior season, people started talking him up in terms of the Heisman Trophy. And that talk grew into the roar after the eighth game of the season, when Steve passed for a pair of scores to set an NCAA record for most consecutive games throwing a touchdown pass (19), and then with 11 clicks left on the clock, scrambled in for the score that carried the Cougars to a thrilling 38–34 comeback win over Utah State.

Steve, who set 13 NCAA records, including highest percentage of passes completed in a season (71.39); most total yards gained per game in a season (395.1); and most passes completed in a season (306); and was a consensus All-American pick, wound up as the Heisman runner-up, behind Nebraska running back Mike Rozier. But lots of people, including BYU coach LaVell Edwards, weren't convinced that anyone was better than Steve. "He's as good a football player as you'll ever find," declared Edwards. "I think the amazing thing about Steve is that he has come farther quicker than anyone I've ever seen. He's one of the most dominating performers you'll ever see."

Gil Brandt, the Dallas Cowboys' superscout, rated Steve at the top of his list, too. "He has tremendous movement and a good, accurate arm. He's got good speed, and he carries that entire football team. He's better than any of the quarterbacks they've had at BYU, and he's the guy I'd like to have in Dallas."

When Steve was asked which pro team he'd like to play for, he just shrugged. "Whatever comes will come. I don't worry about it. I think about things like graduation and law school," said Steve, who was an Academic All-American and a National Football Hall of Fame Scholar Athlete. "Those things I can control. But with the draft, you know, there isn't much choice. You get picked and you go play."

3

There Must Be Some Way Out Of Here

As it turned out, though, Steve did have a choice, because in 1984 an upstart operation, the United States Football League, was in existence and bidding against the NFL for select players such as Steve.

Steve reportedly had a four-year, $4-million offer on the table from the Cincinnati Bengals, the team with the top pick in the NFL's 1984 draft. And he also had an offer from the Los Angeles Express, one of the teams from the USFL, that was somewhere in the stratosphere.

While Steve weighed the offers and the opportunities, he was bombarded with phone calls from some very high profile people who hoped to influence his decision. Donald Trump, one of the richest men in America and the owner of the USFL's New Jersey Generals, was one of the people who tried to persuade Steve to join the new league. Steve was also courted by Pete Roselle, who was the commissioner of the NFL, and Roger Staubach, a Hall of Famer who had been Steve's favorite player when "Roger the Dodger" was the scrambling signal caller for the Dallas Cowboys.

In the end, Steve decided to sign with the Express so that he could become an instant starter, rather than accept the offer from the Bengals, which would have, in all likelihood, turned Steve into a bench warmer for a couple of seasons. Steve was also attracted by LA's coaching staff, which included John Hadl, a former All-Pro quarterback, and Sid Gillman, who had long been considered one of the game's top offensive innovators. Steve thought that one way or the other, either through a merger of the two leagues or a collapse of the USFL, he would eventually wind up in the NFL. But he reasoned that he'd be a lot better prepared for that opportunity if he had the on-the-job training that he would receive with the Express rather than serving as a backup in Cincinnati.

In March of 1984, Steve was scheduled to fly to San Francisco, meet his agent, and sign the contract with William Olderburg, the 46-year-old owner of the Express.

But as soon as Steve stepped out of his 19-year-old Oldsmobile, the car that his teammates at BYU had dubbed "The Tuna Boat", he seemed to step right into an episode of "THE TWILIGHT ZONE."

After he had parked the jalopy in the airport parking lot in Provo, Steve was whisked away in Olderburg's private jet to San Francisco, where he was picked up by a chauffeur driving a Rolls Royce and driven to a downtown office building which housed the headquarters of Investment Mortgage International, Inc., a multinational company that had been founded by Olderburg.

Steve and his agent, Lee Steinberg, thought they were going to Olderburg's plush office to merely put the finishing touches on a contract that had already been negotiated between LeGrande Young and Don Klosterman, the general manager of the Express. The meeting, though, grew tense and drew out into the early hours of the next morning as Steinberg, concerned about the staying power of the USFL, insisted that Olderburg guarantee a substantial portion of the contract with a large cash payment.

Olderburg, enraged, rolled up a large wad of bills and threw them at Steve and his agent, while he screamed, "Here's all the guarantees you'll need."

At one point, long after the sun had set over the Golden Gate Bridge, Olderburg grew so irritated that he walked over to Steve and jabbed a finger in his chest while telling Steve what he thought about his refusal to sign the contract exactly as Olderburg had drawn it up. "If you touch me one more time," growled Steve, "I'll deck you."

A few minutes later, Olderburg's security guards were escorting Steve and Lee Steinberg out of the office building and into a gray and misty San Francisco morning.

But eventually the deal did get done and Steve signed what was, at that time – and by a large amount – the largest contract in the history of team sports: a $40 million gusher that was scheduled to go on pumping money into Steve's bank account through the year 2027.

"I almost fainted that day. I really did," said Steve, who immediately endowed a $183,000 scholarship to BYU as a way of thanking the school for the education he had received and the opportunity that he had been given to showcase his skills on the gridiron. "I remember talking to a reporter from Channel 5 in Los Angeles, and I had to hold on to a rail. It was unbelievable."

Suddenly, Steve was identified in headlines all around the country as "The $40 Million Man." "I don't think Steve was prepared for it, and I don't know how I could have prepared him for it," said Steinberg. "It wasn't treated like a sports story. It was a major cultural phenomenon."

The amount of money was so staggering and the publicity so unrelenting and, oftentimes, unflattering, that Steve went into a shell, and thought about canceling the contract. "The money just overwhelmed him," said Steve's dad. "The money became his nemesis and he continued to live as though he didn't have it. He almost decided not to go to Los Angeles."

Steve finally decided to report. But he got off to a slow start and missed the first six games of the 1984 season because the USFL played a spring schedule and Steve wanted to finish his classes and graduate on time. Steve did start 12 games, though, and under the circumstances, turned in a decent rookie season and became the first player in pro football history to rush for 100 yards and pass for 300 yards in the same game.

The Express quickly started running on a local track, though, as Olderburg's financial empire touched a third rail and went up in smoke. The following year, the franchise was in such sorry shape that the USFL had to step in and take over the team and meet its payroll. But the turmoil continued to take its toll, and the Express was evicted from its training camp center due to unpaid bills.

The last straw for Steve, though, was the fiasco surrounding the 1985 season finale. The team, in full uniform, boarded a bus for a 45-minute ride to a junior college stadium for a game against the Arizona Wranglers. Halfway to the field, though, the driver pulled the bus over to the side of the road and announced that he was going to sit there until he was paid for the trip. Although some of the players were ready to sit out the game, the team finally decided to pass around the hat and pay the driver with their own money.

Due to the franchise's dire financial straits, the team hadn't bothered to sign any replacements for players who had been injured late in the season. So at the start of the game, the Express was down to one healthy running back, Mel Gray, who has since gone on to become an All-Pro kick returner for the Detroit Lions. When Gray went down with an injury in the third quarter, Steve was pressed into service as the team's one and only running back. "It felt like a high school game out there," said Steve. "I was waiting for the cheerleaders to come running off the bus."

After two undistinguished seasons in a second-rate league, Steve wanted out so badly he paid more than a million dollars to get released from his contract. The USFL was in total disarray and about to sink into oblivion and Steve was anxious to give his stalled career a jump-start. "You want to feel like you're going somewhere, accomplishing something," said Steve. "That's where it was really hard."

Unfortunately, life wasn't about to get any better any time soon for Steve, because his NFL rights were held by the Tampa Bay Buccaneers, which was as low as you could go and still be in the NFL.

Steve, who signed a 6-year, $5.4-million contract with the Bucs in the summer of 1985, wound up wasting two more years of his pro career. The Bucs, as usual, were a terrible team during Steve's term with them, managing to win only four of 32 games during the 1985–86 seasons. And while Steve's play didn't set the league on fire, it was hard to spark a team with such low morale. A lot of the players just went sleepwalking through their assignments.

"One time we were playing the Bears, and one of our coaches looked me right in the eye and said, 'Look, Steve, I know everybody's kind of quit on you here. This is the kind of game where you could really get hurt. Be careful out there.' I couldn't believe it. How can you enter a game thinking like that?"

On that Tampa Bay team with Steve was veteran Steve DeBerg, who had quarterbacked the Bill Walsh–coached San Francisco 49ers before he had been beaten out by Joe Montana. DeBerg realized that

Steve, a diamond in the rough, required a master jeweler who could supply the polish that would allow Steve's talent to shine through. "What Steve needed for his career to go to the next level was to be exposed to some top NFL coaching," said DeBerg. "I told him the perfect place for him was San Francisco, with Bill Walsh."

Confidentially, while DeBerg was advising Steve to find some way to get to San Francisco, Sid Gillman, one of Steve's coaches with the Express, was singing his praises to Bill Walsh.

"He's the finest quarterback athlete I've ever seen," raved Gillman, who has seen all the great quarterbacks. "And he can throw any kind of pass that needs to be thrown. He can drill it in there, he can lay it in, he can touch it in – and on top of that he has tremendous intelligence."

Walsh took a close-up look at Steve and quickly saw the vast potential that had been covered up by the ineptness of the Bucs. "Tampa couldn't protect the passer, plus they were running a dated offense," declared Walsh. "So Steve looked bad there." Walsh realized that Steve could become a topflight QB if he was on a good team and received quality coaching, so Walsh executed a swap that brought Steve to the 49ers for the 1987 season.

4

Waiting in the Wings

Steve's arrival in San Francisco didn't set off any fireworks or bring him instant stardom. For one thing, Steve had to learn the 49ers' offensive system, a system that requires pinpoint passing and exquisite timing between the quarterback and his receivers. For another thing, Walsh had to perform a salvage job on Steve, who had spent the previous four years submerged in football oblivion.

"When he came to San Francisco, Steve was pretty shaken up related to his self-confidence and shaken up as to what he might be able to accomplish on a football field," recalled Walsh, who is now the head coach at Stanford University. "Steve had spent a number of seasons just being totally frustrated and maligned."

Finally, the 49ers already had a starting quarterback, a fellow by the name of Joe Montana, who is widely considered to be the greatest signal caller ever to lace up a pair of cleats. Montana had already led the 49ers to two Super Bowl wins before Steve arrived in San Francisco, and he would lead them to two more over the next four years while Steve waited in the wings.

During the course of the next four seasons as Montana's backup, Steve absorbed as much as he could by practicing diligently and watching Montana smoothly run one of the most efficient offensive machines ever assembled. And whenever Montana was injured, which wasn't often, Steve would step in and produce mostly spectacular results. In his limited playing time, which amounted to something less than a full season spread over the four years, Steve wound up throwing for over 2,500 yards, including 23 touchdowns and only six interceptions, while contributing another 659 yards and four touchdowns on the ground.

Steve started to show that he could turn into something special during his first season in San Francisco when he brought down the Bears with four touchdown passes. The following season, in a game against Minnesota, Steve put on another prime-time display, which included a 73-yard TD toss to wide receiver John Taylor, and an almost unbelievable 49-yard broken field run that left a string of Viking defenders grasping for air and falling to the ground. The TD jaunt, with 1:58 left in the game, lifted the 49ers to a 24–21 win and helped earned Steve the NFC Offensive Player of the Week Award. "On a show we did recently, we called that run the best in football over the last 25 years," said Steve Sabol, the president of NFL Films.

But those magical moments were spread too thinly over the four years that Steve had played caddie to Montana. So by the end of the 1990 season, a season in which Steve sat and watched while a healthy Montana started all but one game, Steve was ready to consider leaving the 49ers and joining a team that needed a starting quarterback. "I just wanted to get on the field," said Steve as he recalled that frustrating time. "I just couldn't take it anymore." It had been eight years since Steve had started out in pro ball and the sands of his football time were starting to fill the bottom of the jar. The dilemma for Steve, though, was that he liked San Francisco and felt that the 49ers' offensive schemes were perfectly suited to his quarterbacking skills. So after a lot of soul-searching and discussions with his agent, Lee Steinberg, Steve decided to stay put for the time being. "My mission ever since I got here was to be ready to play spectacular football, not just substitute football," said Steve. "Part of the crazy drive about being here and not wanting to go elsewhere, even as Joe kept going and going, was that there is a benchmark of championships here that there is nowhere else. I just want to keep that tradition going. That's the real test for me."

5

Nightmare

Steve finally got the chance to take the test when an injury to Montana's right elbow put him on the shelf for the 1991 season. This was the opportunity that Steve had dreamed about for a long time, but it quickly turned into the most trying nightmare that he had ever experienced.

As soon as Montana's situation became public, it seemed as though the entire San Francisco Bay Area went into mourning. There was an unmistakable sense of loss, as if something precious and irreplaceable had been taken from them. And Montana's replacement became a convenient if irrational target for their terrible disappointment.

In a way, and up to a point, the reaction was understandable, even to Steve. Montana, with his four Super Bowl rings, had become bigger than life. It wasn't just the winning that elevated Montana to the level of a living legend, there was also his cool and elegant style, and his remarkable ability to bring the team from behind in the fourth quarter, and to do it more often than any other quarterback who had ever played the game.

Lost in the glitter of Montana's true greatness, though, were the seasons that he struggled, the games that the 49ers lost and the times that Joe didn't get it done. It was as though everyone in San Francisco was living in a fairy-tale world in which time would always stand still and Montana would always be leading the 49ers to last-second victories and Super Bowl championships.

It's unlikely that anyone could have taken Montana's place and not been treated as an intruder in that world of make-believe. It might have helped, though, if Steve had gotten the 49ers off to a quick start. It also might have helped if Steve's frantic, scrambling style wasn't so different from the cool, patient approach that Montana had developed. And what might have helped most of all was if Montana had supported Steve instead of going out of his way to let everyone in the Bay Area know that he didn't consider Steve to be one of his best buddies. But none of that happened, and Steve didn't get a whole lot of help in struggling through that trying season.

Although Steve put up strong enough numbers to be named the NFL Offensive Player of the Month for October, the 49ers as a team weren't performing anywhere close to expectations. The year before, with Montana at the helm, the Niners had sailed to an NFL-best 14-2 record for the second consecutive season, and were on their way to an unprecedented third straight Super Bowl appearance until a fourth-quarter fumble by running back Roger Craig in the NFC championship game gave the Giants a chance to kick a game-winning field goal with only .04 left on the clock. But through the first half of the 1991 season, those same 49ers were stalled at 4-4, and all the fingers were pointed at Steve. The media and the 49ers fans were being hysterical and hypercritical, and even some of Steve's teammates were blaming him for the team's fall from grace.

After one tough loss, the frustrations and whispered regrets about what would have been if only Montana was healthy surfaced with a vengeance as linebacker Charles Haley went ballistic and blasted Steve in the 49ers' locker room. Then Jerry Rice, the 49ers' All-Pro wide receiver poured oil on the fire when he evaluated Steve by saying, "He's a great *running* quarterback." The implication, of course, was that Steve scrambled too often instead of sitting in the pocket and passing the ball, which was true. But saying it in public didn't do anything to boost Steve's confidence or to get the media and the fans off of Steve's back.

It would take time and experience before Steve would feel comfortable enough to realize that his over-reliance on his feet was upsetting the receivers and disrupting the offensive schemes. Through experience he would learn to stay in the pocket more and let the receivers finish running their routes. And he would also learn that when he scrambled he should keep his head up and his eyes downfield, looking to throw first and run only when none of his receivers were open.

But no one seemed to be willing to give Steve that time.

In the ninth game of the season, Steve, after throwing a team record 97-yard scoring strike to wide receiver John Taylor, went down and out with an injury to his left knee. Third-string quarterback Steve Bono then stepped in and after losing one outing led the 49ers to five straight wins. In the last two wins, Bono threw six touchdown passes while leading the Niners to Montana-like come-from-behind rallies, the first of which earned him NFC Offensive Player of the Week honors. Although Steve had been dressed and ready to play in those two games, George Seifert, who had replaced Walsh as head coach prior to the start of the 1989 season, kept him on the bench and let Bono play out his hot hand. It wasn't until Bono went out with a knee injury of his own in the third quarter of the following week, that Steve got back on the field. Steve finished out that win for Bono and then closed out the 1991 season by throwing three TD passes and running for a fourth as he led the Niners to a 52–14 bashing of the Bears.

Steve's hot finish allowed him to compile a league-high 101.8 QB rating. Only 12 other quarterbacks in the history of the NFL had ever topped the century mark, including, of course, Joe Montana, who had done it three times and who also owned the highest single-season rating, 112.4, as well as the all-time highest career rating.

Despite the uniqueness of Steve's personal accomplishment, the bottom line was that the 49ers, with a 10-6 record, had finished out of the playoff picture for the first time since 1982, and most of the blame was directed at Steve. Although 10-6 records are usually enough for a team to make it into postseason play, Steve was more than willing to accept his fair share of the responsibility for the 49ers' unexpectedly early start into the offseason. "To be a great QB, your team must be great," said Steve. "That's what your job is." But it was unfair and inaccurate to lay all of the team's failure at Steve's feet. And the sad irony of Steve's statistical leadership was that in the eyes of most San Franciscans – including a majority of his teammates – Steve wasn't a leader at all and no better than third on the QB chart behind the still-injured Montana and Bono.

It wasn't only a question of not making the playoffs, though.

There was also the fact that Steve hadn't demonstrated an ability to bring the team from behind as Montana had done with such breathtaking regularity, and as Bono had done twice in only six starts.

The critics also carped that Steve had scrambled too often, disrupting the team's finely tuned passing game and upsetting Jerry Rice, who was angry about not getting the ball delivered to him as well or as often as he would have liked; the way, it seemed, that Montana had always delivered it.

6

It's My Job

During the offseason, when it seemed that Montana was headed for a complete recovery, and with Bono available as a more than capable backup, the 49ers' high command decided that Steve was expendable. "Remember where we were in March of 1992," said 49ers president Carmen Policy. "The coaches said that Joe was throwing better than he had in years. And the prospect of Steve Young being an unhappy camper would have been a distraction to the team."

Ultimately, no team came up with the players and draft choices that the 49ers considered to be fair compensation for Steve, although a trade with the Raiders involving wide receiver Tim Brown came tantalizingly close to being completed.

It turned out to be the best trade that the 49ers never made, because Montana's injury didn't heal in time for the 1992 season, and after a spirited competition in the preseason games, Seifert named Steve as the team's opening-day starter.

Although Steve had gotten the nod from Seifert, most San Franciscans, as well as a majority of the 49ers, thought that Bono had outplayed Steve during the previous year and in the preseason games. But everyone was just hoping that Steve was only a temporary stand-in anyway, someone to hold down the fort until Montana could ride into action and lead the Niners' charge back to the top of the standings.

Steve's season got off to a shaky start when he suffered a concussion on the fifth play of the opening game. While Steve's head was ringing like an unanswered telephone, Bono took over and calmly hit on two scoring passes that spearheaded the 49ers to a 31–14 win over the Giants. The following week, the Niners bowed to the Bills 34–31, despite a spectacular performance by Steve, who threw for a career-high 449 yards and three touchdowns.

Instead of concentrating on Steve's awesome accomplishments,

Bay Area critics claimed that Montana would have found a way to win the game. The following week, Steve threw for a pair of TD's and ran for a third in leading the Niners to a 31–14 win over the New York Jets. In the locker room, though, one reporter asked Steve if he felt responsible for the broken leg that John Taylor suffered when he had been hit while leaping for a high pass that Steve had thrown — as if Montana had thrown only perfect passes that receivers never had to jump or stretch to reach.

And even after Steve had led the 49ers on a five-game winning streak capped by a 56-point explosion against the Falcons and been selected as the NFL's Offensive Player of the Month for October, the long shadow of Montana continued to hang over him. A chorus of critics, led by Jerry Rice, claimed that Steve wasn't throwing enough to Rice, Montana's favorite target and, arguably, the greatest receiver to ever catch a football.

Although Steve was upset and hurt by the unrelenting criticism, even in the face of a five-game winning streak, he reacted with astonishing poise and even put a positive spin on his predicament. "It's part of enjoying the process of life," claimed Steve. "It's not only enjoying when things go your way, but enjoying times when it's a little bit tougher."

The flu knocked Steve out of the next game, a loss to Phoenix which dropped their record to 6-2 at the halfway point of the season. But Steve came back strong and KO'd the Falcons once again by throwing for three TD's in a 41–3 rout at Atlanta. Falcons defensive end Tim Green was going to be sleeping a lot better knowing that Steve was headed out of town. "On Sunday morning when you have to play Young, you wake up with a sickening feeling and a headache. I can honestly say those are the only times I've ever approached a game conceding that an opposing player is going to make big plays no matter what we do."

The following week, Steve took a giant step toward winning the confidence of his teammates when he threw a pair of fourth-quarter TD passes that rallied the Niners to a 21–20 win over New Orleans and broke a first-place tie with the Saints. "Those last drives, he was just as calm as Joe ever was," said veteran guard Guy McIntyre.

Steve stayed so hot that he finished the season with a league-leading 107.0 quarterback rating – and became the first player in NFL history to lead the league in consecutive seasons with a QB rating over 100. Steve, who also led the league in touchdown passes and completion percentage, capped his spectacular season by being named the NFL's MVP and the Player of the Year by both *Sports Illustrated* and *The Sporting News*. But of all the honors that Steve gathered, the one that meant the most was the Len Eshmont Award, which is voted on by the 49ers players and given to the player that they select as the most inspirational and courageous. "When you see what Steve's gone through and how he's hung in there when things didn't look real good, it says a lot for Steve's character," noted linebacker Michael Walter. And even Jerry Rice had climbed on Steve's bandwagon. "He's had an MVP year, no doubt about it. He has an attitude now, you can just look at him whenever he takes the field, he's got confidence in himself."

It had been a long time coming, but Steve had arrived at where he wanted to be. "This is something I always knew I would do, once I had opportunity to grow into the position."

Most importantly, Steve had piloted the 49ers to an NFL-best 14-2 record, including a season-ending 8-0 run that put them on a roll heading into the playoffs.

Steve's first postseason start came at home against Washington on a Candlestick Park field that had been turned into a semiswamp by a week of steady rain. Steve, though, overcame the slippery conditions and shot the Niners into a 17–3 halftime lead on a pair of scoring strikes, a five-yard toss to John Taylor and a 16-yard dart to tight end Brent Jones. In the second half, however, a stalled offense and two fumbles by Steve allowed Washington to turn the fourth quarter into a 17–13 nailbiter.

Over on the sidelines, the 49ers' offense was in a state of disarray. "Everyone's yelling and screaming," related tackle Harris Barton. "Some guys are going over to Steve and saying, 'Hey, brother, let's get going.' Others are staying away from him. There's near-panic out there."

As Steve led the 49ers back onto the field, Montana, who had finally returned to action in the second half of the season's final game, took off his jacket and started warming up. "It was only a precautionary move," said Seifert afterward. "I thought Steve might have been banged up diving for that fumble on the previous possession."

Steve was fine, as he demonstrated by taking the 49ers on a time-consuming drive and positioning the field goal that stretched the Niners' lead to 20–13, which is just how the game ended. Afterward, a lot of the San Francisco reporters seemed more interested in Steve's turnovers and the Montana angle than they did in Steve coming through with the win. But Steve wasn't interested. "The big thing I'll focus on is the big drive and we'll just go on from there. I'm here now and it's my job."

Troy Aikman, the quarterback of the Dallas Cowboys team that the 49ers were about to meet in the NFC championship game, also thought that Steve had passed all the tests. "He earned the MVP award and he deserves to be playing," declared Troy. "He's handled the situation with Joe Montana in an admirable fashion, and I think he's answered all the critics."

What Steve couldn't quite answer, though, was the firepower of Aikman and his Cowboy teammates. Steve might have guessed that it wasn't his day when, on the third offensive play of the game, he connected with Rice on an apparent 63-yard touchdown pass, only to have it called back because of a holding call on Guy McIntyre. "It would have been a heck of a start," lamented Steve. "That one was tougher as the game wore on because we kept thinking about it."

Steve had the 49ers even at the half, 10–10, but Aikman put the Cowboys ahead for good with a third-quarter touchdown pass to Emmitt Smith. The 49ers did make a fourth-quarter run at the Cowboys as Steve directed a masterly 93-yard drive which he ended with a TD toss to Rice that cut the Dallas lead to 24–20 with 4:22 left in the game. The 49ers were hoping to shut down the Cowboys and get the ball back in Steve's hands. But Aikman shot those plans down with a four-play TD drive that salted the game away and made the final score 30–20.

The loss was very hard for Steve to accept. "It's tough to put into words. Here we really expected to go all the way this year. There aren't a lot of pats on the back at this point. Right now, it hurts." But after taking a little time to recover and to think about how far he'd come and how much he had accomplished, Steve couldn't help but smile. "Now, I can't wait, I just can't wait until next year."

7

Roller Coaster Ride

Steve's life in 1993 was like a year-long roller coaster ride, starting in the offseason when the 49ers' management couldn't seem to decide whether Steve, who had led the NFL in passing the previous two seasons, or Joe Montana, who had played one half in those two seasons, would go to training camp as the team's first-string quarterback. After a series of contradictory statements from George Seifert and Carmen Policy that made the Niners' management look inept, the situation was finally resolved when Montana was traded to the Kansas City Chiefs for a No. 1 draft pick.

While the three-ring circus was being played out in San Francisco, Steve was back at BYU, trying to concentrate on his last semester of law school classes. Although Steve was stung by the team's refusal to say that he was No. 1, despite his two passing titles and MVP award, he never took any slaps at the team's management or at Montana. "I understand how the organization was feeling. Here, after all, is a guy who has led them to four Super Bowl wins. It was a very emotional situation, and I think everybody tried to do the right thing.

"But when this is all over, I may be able to say that I had the strangest career in pro football history."

Once Steve arrived in training camp, he was up after signing a five-year $26.75-million contract that made him the highest paid player in the NFL until Aikman signed an even bigger deal later in the year. But a few weeks later, he was down after breaking a bone in his left thumb.

The thumb, which was swollen to the size of a sausage, caused Steve to start the 1993 season in erratic fashion. Over the first four games, Steve threw eight interceptions, one more than he had thrown in all of 1993, and only six touchdown passes. Over the next seven games, with his thumb nearly healed, Steve was almost unstoppable as he threw for 16 TD's and only two INT's, while posting a QB rating of 122.7.

It was during that seven-game streak that Steve reached the zone that only the great quarterbacks ever attain. "The field seemed to open up and the players seemed to slow down. I knew where everybody was without looking, sometimes without even thinking about it."

Steve's teammates also noticed that he had taken his game to a higher level. "His recognition, his timing, his quick decisions remind you of Montana," said offensive tackle Steve Wallace. "He's no longer just a great athlete playing quarterback, he's a great quarterback in his own right."

Steve had also grown more mature and learned to accept the fact that mistakes are an inevitable part of life. "You're going to make mistakes sometimes. You just can't get caught up in them." And he also grew a thicker skin so as to take the sting out of unjustified criticism. "You have to learn to ignore what people say when they don't know what they're talking about. You can't get upset about it."

Although Steve cooled down over the final five games of the regular season, he still finished with a 101.5 QB rating and became the only player to lead the NFL in passing and break the century mark in three successive seasons. Along the way, Steve completed a team-record 183 passing attempts without an interception, and became the first QB in 49ers history to throw for over 4,000 yards in a single season.

"He is the most effective quarterback playing the game today and my choice as the best simply because he's such a brilliant athlete," declared Bill Walsh, when asked to compare Steve and Troy Aikman. "Both are absolutely gifted athletes. Rarely are there more than one or two players like this at any one time."

"They are it," added Fritz Schurmur, the defensive coordinator of the Phoenix Cardinals. "No question about it. How do you choose between them? They're either one and two, or two and one."

Although Steve appreciates what he's accomplished and the awards and the praise that he's earned, he never allows himself to be too content with where he's at. He always wants to be aiming himself at the next target. "Let's say I acknowledge it's a great feeling and then I push on, so that there's always an edge to things."

Although Steve had finished the 1993 season in a mini-slump and the Niners had dropped three of their last four games to finish at 10–6, they had won the NFC Western Division, and Steve wasn't about to allow the San Francisco media to downplay the team's chances in the playoffs. "I am not going to let myself or the rest of the team feel like we're in a jam. We've overcome mistakes all year long."

Then the Niners went out and backed up Steve's words by demolishing the Giants in a divisional playoff game, and they did it against one of the stingiest defenses in the NFL. Steve, who completed 17 of 22 passes for 226 yards, directed the 49ers to scoring drives on four of their first five possessions, while running back Ricky Watters, who rushed for five scores, set an NFL postseason record for touchdowns in a single game. "Our offensive line was awesome, I mean really awesome," said Steve with a happy grin. And the much maligned Niners defense, which had been ranked 28th in the league against the run, stuffed the Giants' No. 1 ranked running game.

But Steve and the Niners came crashing down to earth the following week as they were once again stampeded by the Cowboys in the NFC championship game, 38–21. "I'm trying to keep a stiff upper lip here," said Steve, who didn't take any consolation from his 27 completions or 287 passing yards that were accomplished despite a relentless Dallas defense that constantly kept their rush in Steve's face. "I never would have believed we'd come down here and get beat by this score. They did a great job. We have to earn the right to do this again."

The 49ers' management took immediate steps toward helping the team earn their way back to title contention in 1994 by beefing up their defense. Among the new players are pass-rushing specialist Richard Dent and linebacker Ken Norton, who was the heart and soul of the Dallas defense. With those pieces added to the Niners picture, they should now be in a position to fulfill Steve's dream and make their run to the Super Bowl. As Jerry Rice noted, "You win championships with defense, and that's something Steve hasn't had. You've got to have a great defense just like you have to have a great offense."

When Steve was still playing for the Buccaneers, Sid Gillman made a prediction. "Steve Young is a Super Bowl quarterback," declared Gillman. "I'd bet my life on it. Put him in a good organization that has a good passing concept and I promise you he'll take them to a Super Bowl." 1994 could be the year.

But no matter what happens from here on out, Steve has already established himself as one of the top quarterbacks of all time, and he has the awards and statistics to prove it. In terms of career QB ratings, he trails only Montana, and only by the thinnest of margins, 93.0 to 93.1. He also ranks right behind Montana and right in front of Aikman in career completion percentage.

And while Steve is thoroughly devoted to football and bringing a Super Bowl home to San Francisco, there is a whole lot more to Steve's life than simply passing a ball down the field.

Steve, who spent a lot of his offseasons studying law at BYU, finally received his degree in 1994. At his graduation, Steve reacted with a mixture of seriousness and levity. "This has been a big goal for a lot of years. It hasn't been real easy. But I'm glad I'm educated to do the things I'd like to do. And now at least my dad thinks I'm qualified to do something, like get a real job."

Steve also figured that his law degree could come in handy against blitzing linebackers. "I'll sue for assault and battery on the field," joked Steve. "It won't just be 15 yards; it will be 15 yards and a cash settlement."

The real reason that Steve has worked so hard to become a lawyer, though, is that he has a deep and abiding interest in helping others. "People are in trouble," said Steve. "This huge, ugly system faces them and you're the only way to get people through the maze. If you're ethical and have a lot of care for individual people, you can help. I can help them through a system that is confusing even to me. We have to find a way to reach people, because it's easy to get lost."

Steve has always spent a lot of time and a lot of his money helping others. "The only fun I have with money is to be able to spread it around and do some fun things for people," said Steve, who lives very simply despite all the money that he's earned.

One example of Steve helping others involved a Russian physicist who was teaching a summer course at BYU. Steve heard that the scientist had extremely bad teeth and was in constant pain, but couldn't afford to see a dentist. "Even the dentist said he'd never seen anything like it," said Steve, who took it upon himself to set up the appointment and pay the dentist's bill.

Steve is constantly committing random acts of kindness, like playing Santa Claus at a homeless shelter. While other people may look down their noses at people who have taken a fall, Steve realizes that homeless people aren't lazy and didn't choose that way of life. He knows that those unfortunate people, at least for the time being, have been dealt a blow that's knocked them off their feet. "There's such a misconception about it, that people have done something wrong. But these people — especially the kids — have nowhere else to go," said Steve with the clear understanding that bad times can happen to anyone.

Steve has also spent a lot of time helping Native Americans. "He goes down with me to the reservations to give seminars, helping kids with their self-esteem," related Dale Tingey, director of American Indian Services in Provo. "He shares instances in his life when he's failed and they realize that if he can overcome it, they can, too. And he helps organize fund-raising dinners for scholarships that have sent hundreds of Indian students to college. He has a great love for the people."

In 1992, Steve set up his own charitable operation, called "Forever Young." The Foundation is organized to fund charitable organizations that, "encourage the development, security, strength and spiritual vitality of the family."

"To me, it's people getting along, doing the little things. It's basically the family and then your extended family, which really extends to anyone you come in contact with. That's what matters. You can't change the world, but you can change your little part of it."

Sources

The Daily Oklahoman
The Dallas Cowboys Official Weekly
The Dallas Morning News
Desert News
Fantastic Flyer Magazine
Football Digest
Inside Sports
The Norman Transcript
Sacramento Bee
The Salt Lake City Tribune
San Francisco Chronicle
San Francisco Examiner
San Jose Mercury
Sports Illustrated
Sport Magazine
The Sporting News
Tulsa World

If you want to write to the author, address your letter to:

Richard J. Brenner
c/o East End Publishing
54 Alexander Dr.
Syosset, NY 11791

All letters that require an answer *must* include a self-addressed and stamped envelope.

If you want to write to Troy Aikman address your letter to:

Troy Aikman
c/o Dallas Cowboys
One Cowboys Parkway
Irving, TX 75063-4727

If you want to write to Steve Young address your letter to:

Steve Young
c/o San Francisco 49ers
4949 Centennial Blvd.
Santa Clara, CA 95054

TROY AIKMAN

Birthdate: November 21, 1966
Birthplace: West Covina, California
Height: 6-4   Weight: 222

COLLEGE STATS

| | PASSING | | | | | | | RUSHING | | | |
	ATT.	COMP.	YDS.	PCT.	TD.	INT.	RATING	ATT.	YDS.	AVG.	TD.
1984	20	6	41	.30	0	3	—	12	47	1.5	1
1985	47	27	442	.574	1	1	—	49	191	1.9	0
1987	273	178	2527	.652	17	8	—				
1988	354	228	2771	.644	24	9	—				

NFL REGULAR SEASON STATS

	ATT.	COMP.	YDS.	PCT.	TD.	INT.	RATING	ATT.	YDS.	AVG.	TD.
1989	293	155	1749	52.9	9	18	55.7	38	302	7.9	0
1990	399	226	2579	56.6	11	18	66.6	40	172	4.3	1
1991	363	237	2754	65.3	11	10	86.7	16	5	0.3	1
1992	473	302	3445	63.8	23	14	89.5	37	105	2.8	1
1993	392	271	3100	69.1	15	6	99.0	32	125	3.9	0

NFL POSTSEASON STATS

	ATT.	COMP.	YDS.	PCT.	TD.	INT.	RATING	ATT.	YDS.	AVG.	TD.
1991	16	11	114	68.8	0	1	63.0	2	0	0.0	0
1992	89	61	795	68.5	8	0	126.4	9	38	4.2	0
1993	82	61	686	74.4	5	3	104.4	7	28	4.0	0

STEVEN YOUNG

Birthdate: October 11, 1961
Birthplace: Salt Lake City, Utah
Height: 6-2   Weight: 200

COLLEGE STATS

	ATT.	COMP.	PASSING YDS.	PCT.	TD.	INT.	RATING	RUSHING ATT.	YDS.	AVG.	TD.
1981	112	56	731	.500	5	5	111.6	53	233	4.4	0
1982	367	233	3100	.627	18	18	140.0	144	407	3.6	10
1983	429	306	3902	.713	33	10	168.5	102	144	4.3	8

REGULAR SEASON STATS

	ATT.	COMP.	PASSING YDS.	PCT.	TD.	INT.	RATING	RUSHING ATT.	YDS.	AVG.	TD.
1984 (USFL)	310	179	2361	.577	10	9	80.6	79	515	6.5	7
1985	250	137	1741	.548	6	13	63.1	56	368	6.6	2
1985 (TB)	138	72	935	.522	3	8	56.9	40	233	5.8	1
1986	363	195	2282	.537	8	14	65.5	74	425	3.5	5
1987 (SF)	69	37	570	.536	10	0	120.8	26	190	7.3	1
1988	101	54	680	.535	3	3	72.2	27	184	6.8	1
1989	92	64	1001	.696	8	3	120.8	38	126	3.3	2
1990	62	38	427	.613	2	0	92.6	15	159	10.6	0
1991	279	180	2517	.645	17	8	101.8	66	415	6.3	4
1992	402	268	3465	.667	25	7	107.0	16	106	6.6	1
1993	462	314	4023	.680	29	16	101.5	69	407	5.9	2

POSTSEASON STATS

	ATT.	COMP.	PASSING YDS.	PCT.	TD.	INT.	RATING	RUSHING ATT.	YDS.	AVG.	TD.
1984 (USFL)	67	30	421	.448	1	4	46.0	9	68	7.6	0
1987 (SF)	17	12	158	.706	1	1	94.7	6	72	12.0	1
1988	1	1	-1	.1000	0	0	79.2	3	1	0.3	0
1989	5	3	26	.600	0	0	73.8	5	5	1.0	0
1990	1	1	25	.1000	0	0	118.8	0	0	0.0	0
1992	65	45	540	.692	3	3	90.5	16	106	6.6	1
1993	67	44	513	.657	1	1	87.5	10	55	5.5	1

If you enjoyed this book you might want to order some of our other exciting titles:

BASKETBALL SUPERSTARS ALBUM 1995, Richard J. Brenner. Includes 16 full-color pages, and mini-bios of the game's top superstars, plus career and all time stats. 48 pages ($4.50/$5.50 Can.)

SHAQUILLE O'NEAL * LARRY JOHNSON, by Richard J. Brenner. A dual biography of the two brightest young stars in basketball. 96 pages, 10 pages of photos. ($3.50/$4.50 Can.)

MICHAEL JORDAN * MAGIC JOHNSON, by Richard J. Brenner. A dual biography of two of the greatest superstars of all time. 128 pages, 15 dynamite photos. ($3.50/$4.25 Can.)

TROY AIKMAN * STEVE YOUNG, by Richard J. Brenner. A dual biography of the top two quarterbacks in the NFL. 96 pages, 10 pages of photos. ($3.50/$4.50 Can.)

BARRY BONDS * ROBERTO ALOMAR, by Bob Woods. A dual biography of two of the brightest stars in baseball. 96 pages, 10 pages of photos. ($3.50/$4.50 Can.)

MARIO LEMIEUX, by Richard J. Brenner. An exciting biography of one of hockey's all time greats. 96 pages, 10 pages of photos. ($3.50/$4.50 Can.)

THE WORLD SERIES, THE GREAT CONTESTS, by Richard J. Brenner. The special excitement of the Fall Classic is brought to life through seven of the most thrilling Series ever played, including 1993. 176 pages, including 16 action-packed photos. ($3.50/$4.50 Can.)

THE COMPLETE SUPER BOWL STORY, GAMES I-XXVIII, by Richard J. Brenner. The most spectacular moments in Super Bowl history are brought to life, game by game. 224 pages, including 16 memorable photos. ($4.00/$5.00 Can.)

SHAQUILLE O'NEAL, by Richard J. Brenner. An easy-to-read, photo-filled biography especially for younger readers. 32 pages. ($3.25/$4.50 Can.)

MICHAEL JORDAN, by Richard J. Brenner. An easy-to-read, photo-filled biography especially for younger readers. 32 pages. ($3.50/$4.50 Can.)

WAYNE GRETZKY, by Richard J. Brenner. An easy-to-read, photo-filled biography of hockey's greatest player. 32 pages. Revised edition. ($3.25/$4.50 Can.)

PLEASE SEE NEXT PAGE FOR ORDER FORM

ORDER FORM

Payment must accompany all orders. All payments must be in U.S. dollars. Postage and handling is $1.35 per book up to a maximum of $6.75 ($1.75 to a maximum of $8.75 in Canada).
Please send me _____ total books as per the following:

❑ BASKETBALL SUPERSTARS ALBUM 1995
❑ SHAQUILLE O'NEAL * LARRY JOHNSON
❑ MICHAEL JORDAN * MAGIC JOHNSON
❑ TROY AIKMAN * STEVE YOUNG
❑ BARRY BONDS * ROBERTO ALOMAR
❑ MARIO LEMIEUX
❑ THE WORLD SERIES, THE GREAT CONTESTS
❑ THE COMPLETE SUPER BOWL STORY, GAMES I-XXVIII
❑ SHAQUILLE O'NEAL
❑ MICHAEL JORDAN
❑ WAYNE GRETZKY

PRICE OF BOOKS $_____
POSTAGE AND HANDLING $_____
TOTAL PAYMENT ENCLOSED $_____

NAME _____

ADDRESS _____

CITY_____STATE _____ ZIP CODE:_____

COUNTRY_____

Send to: East End Publishing, Ltd., 54 Alexander Drive, Syosset, NY 11791 USA. Dept. WGB. Allow three weeks for delivery. Discounts are available on orders of 25 or more copies. For details, call (516) 364-6383.